W9-ACA-792

CRIME TALK

SOCIAL PROBLEMS AND SOCIAL ISSUES

An Aldine de Gruyter Series of Texts and Monographs

SERIES EDITOR

Joel Best

Southern Illinois University at Carbondale

CRIME TALK

How Citizens Construct a Social Problem

THEODORE SASSON

ALDINE DE GRUYTER
New York

ABOUT THE AUTHOR

Theodore Sasson is Assistant Professor of Sociology and Anthropology at Middlebury College. His research interests are in political sociology and criminology.

ALDINE DE GRUYTER
A division of Walter de Gruyter, Inc.
200 Saw Mill River Road
Hawthorne, New York 10532

This publication is printed on acid free paper

Library of Congress Cataloging-in-Publication Data
Sasson, Theodore, 1965–
    Crime talk : how citizens construct a social problem / Theodore Sasson.
        p.   cm. — (Social problems and social issues)
    Includes bibliographical references and index.
    ISBN 0-202-30547-3 (acid-free paper) 0-202-30546-5 paper
    1. Discourse analysis—Social aspects—United States.   2. Crime—United States.   3. Mass media and language—United States.
    4. United States—Social conditions—1980-   I. Title.   II. Series.
    P302.84.S27   1995
    401'.41—dc20   95-23008
                                                             CIP

Manufactured in the United States of America

10   9   8   7   6   5   4   3   2   1

CONTENTS

PREFACE

Polly Klaas. Car-Jacking. The Long Island Railroad Massacre. Rodney King. The L.A. Riot. Willie Horton. "Wilding" in Central Park. The Chez Vous Roller Rink. The Subway Vigilante. Yusuf Hawkins. Carol Stuart. Lorena Bobbitt. The Menendez Brothers. The "caning" of Michael Fay. O.J. Simpson. John Salvi. Tonya Harding. Heidi Fleiss. . . .

The list could be extended almost indefinitely. The public arena in which American political culture is reproduced overflows with images of crime, violence, and punishment. These images fuel the daily production of analytical discourse: Newspaper columns, magazines articles, radio talk-shows, television "special reports," brim with argument and debate about the sources of urban violence and its remedies. What are the contours of this public debate? What do ordinary people think about the issue? What is the significance of the prominent place crime occupies in American public life?

Answering these questions is the chief aim of this book. Because crime is such a salient issue, how people think about it is of considerable importance. This sentiment is widely shared among scholars and political analysts, thus, as we shall see, the territory I cover is well traveled. The contributions of previous visitors, however, have tended to be theoretically rich, but empirically poor. This book is an attempt to redistribute the wealth.

It is also a case study and hence potentially of broader theoretical significance. Crime, following Gusfield (1981), is a *public problem,* therefore exploring how it is interpreted for, and by ordinary people can inform a larger theoretical interest in the dynamics of the public sphere. The book can thus contribute to our understanding of the relationship between what Edelman (1988) calls the "political spectacle," and the consciousness of regular people.

If dusted for fingerprints, the book would reveal the following contributions. Deborah Grant suggested that I write a book about the politics of crime and persuaded me to stick with the project through its many mutations. Bill Gamson offered guidance and inspiration at every turn.

His fingerprints, a bit faint due to his aversion to heavy-handedness, will be evident on every page. Charles Pinderhughes, facilitator of the black discussion groups, brought to the project unflagging commitment and expert judgment. Rose Miller transcribed more than twenty often chaotic discussions with patience and precision. Members of the Boston College Media Research and Action Project provided feedback at the early stages of the project. Lew Coser, Charlie Derber, Diane Vaughan, Stephen Pfohl and Eve Spangler offered guidance and encouragement throughout. Piers Beirne provided important bibliographic assistance. Katherine Beckett and Joel Best read a complete draft of the manuscript and offered useful criticism, suggestions for revision and kind words to keep me going. Marshall Levin did the painstaking job of preparing the manuscript for publication. Finally, Margaret Nelson, Burke Rochford, Ellen Oxfeld, David Napier and Jean Burfoot of the Department of Sociology and Anthropology at Middlebury College created a supportive environment for the final stage of writing.

The research that resulted in this book received generous financial support from Boston College, the National Science Foundation (SES 9200692), the National Institute of Justice (93–IJ–CX–0005) and the Middlebury College Faculty Professional Development Fund. Although I hope the book finds favor with these sponsors, I am obliged to note that it does not necessarily reflect their viewpoints.

I owe a debt of gratitude to Chris Hayes and Jerry Smart of the Boston Police Department's Neighborhood Crime Watch Program. Without their early and continuous assistance, the research for this project and related work would have been immeasurably more difficult.

Finally, although their names and the names of their streets appear in the text as pseudonyms, I owe a debt of gratitude to the Bostonians who gave so generously of their time and their thoughts. The crime prevention light bulbs they took home from the peer group discussions were small thanks indeed for their contribution to the study.

* * * * *

The book is dedicated, with love, to Deborah Grant and our new son Aryeh Grant-Sasson. Aryeh had the good sense to wait until the moment I finished the final draft to begin his journey into the world. He now sleeps in my lap as I type these words. Miracle of miracles, there is no greater reward.

Theodore Sasson

FOREWORD

Crime pays—for Republicans and conservatives in American politics. *Crime Talk* outlines the conventional wisdom on why this is so. In the absence of the Cold War, the threat of the violent criminal provides a substitute symbolic enemy against whom conservatives "can rally middle Americans in a common struggle." At the same time, this struggle diverts attention and resources away from competing issues on the public agenda, issues that "imply a need for income redistribution or governmental initiatives." The image of the enemy—the violent criminal—has the additional advantage of providing a hidden image of the "black" violent criminal whose content can be decoded in this way by the intended audience while providing the users of the image with plausible deniability of any racial intent. Through this device, the crime issue provides a wedge to create continuing tensions in the Democrats' interracial coalition. Finally—and the part of the argument that *Crime Talk* engages most directly—most ordinary Americans, regardless of party affiliation, are much closer in their opinions to the law and order arguments of conservatives than to the blocked opportunities arguments of liberals.

Furthermore, crime is an issue that is not going away. Pouring more money into police and prisons has been manifestly unsuccessful in the past; crime rates have remained more or less stable. More prisons and police will not reduce crime in any significant way and certainly not enough to remove the strong sense of personal insecurity and vulnerability among most people in cities such as Boston, where Sasson's discussion participants lived. For politicians who choose to ride it, this horse has legs. There is every reason to expect crime to remain a central issue in American politics for at least the next decade.

How much do ordinary Americans share the ideas promoted by conservative frames on crime? *Crime Talk* examines the existing evidence and shows it is equivocal and full of unexplained, apparent contradictions. Sasson assesses the conventional wisdom here with data much richer and deeper than anything previously available. No doubt he would have liked to find that the conventional wisdom was wrong and misleading—indeed, the very choice of term presages that outcome. I hope I won't spoil the ending too much if I tell you up front that he is honest and courageous enough to admit that much of his evidence not only confirms the conventional wisdom in many respects but illuminates the reasons why certain frames have such a powerful appeal for ordinary people while others are especially weak. After reading this account, one can easily imagine the justifiable glee of conservatives when a conventional liberal politician mouths phrases about "poverty" as the root cause of crime. This is the chosen arena for a symbolic contest on the crime issue where conservatives are confident of victory.

So is it nothing but woe for progressives on the crime issue in American politics? *Crime Talk* addresses this question only very briefly in the last few pages but the book as a whole locates exactly where the major opportunity lies. Sasson describes the *Social Breakdown* frame in Chapter 4. This frame, emphasizing the breakdown of the normative order more generally, can take a conservative or progressive flavor. The former version puts more emphasis on the breakdown of the family and the resultant failure to transmit family values of self-discipline and personal responsibility; the latter, on the breakdown of community values of neighborhood and helping others, the breakdown of civic virtue.

While the *Social Breakdown* frame does not fare quite as well in media discourse as its major rival, *Faulty System,* it is extremely powerful in popular discourse. *Crime Talk* reports that "most elements of *Social Breakdown* were broadly resonant with virtually all of the discussion participants." They articulate in varying ways a sense of general breakdown of order and authority, "a kind of societal unraveling," but they have little to say on the sources of this breakdown. Here is an opportunity for arguments about structural causes to play a role in people's understanding of crime issues and to justify policies that emphasize prevention over punishment.

While *Social Breakdown* can take a conservative form, it is not a law and order frame that looks to tougher punishment and more police and prisons as solutions. It is not a progressive frame, either, but one that provides much more favorable turf for progressives to engage in a symbolic contest over how to deal with crime. Even the conservative version suggests preventive measures that will strengthen the family. Once the debate has shifted from punishment and deterrence to what are the most effective ways of reversing the social breakdown, progressives are on much more promising grounds. A progressive version of this frame, which emphasizes the rebuilding of neighborhood and community, and civic responsibility at the local level, can articulate very well with the ways that ordinary Americans understand crime issues. And policy measures that support these goals can win support in an issue arena that has been dominated by conservatives.

In the end, *Crime Talk* offers hope. Yes, there is woe to those conventional liberals who would continue to struggle against the conservative *Faulty System* frame with an enfeebled *Blocked Opportunities* alternative. But there is hope for progressives who would build on the powerful appeal of *Social Breakdown,* articulating its appeals to the rebuilding of community and emphasizing policies that would do this. Anyone who is serious about this project could make no better beginning than reading Sasson's nuanced and subtle account of how ordinary Americans talk about crime.

William A. Gamson

INTRODUCTION

SCENE: *A living room in a Boston neighborhood*
Group: *Jacob's Lane*
Cast:

Laura, *a homemaker and high school graduate, white, in her 40s.*
Carol, *a graduate student, white, in her 40s.*
Alex, *a TV producer and college graduate, white, in his 40s.*
Geraldine, *a homemaker and high school graduate, white, in her 60s.*

Facilitator: What crimes are you most concerned about?

Laura: The one I'm most concerned with is being mugged or raped, or worse, murdered.

Carol: I feel exactly the same way as Laura. I'm also afraid because I have children who are on their own a lot, that something will happen to them. Both my sons are in positions where they're in the city. And I'm terrified that something will happen to them. I mean they're not babies, but I'm just terrified that somebody's gonna walk up and say, "Give me your money." My kids don't carry money. Or "Give me your jacket." My older one would strip down to his skin happily giving his clothes away. But my little one, my younger son, I'm terrified that, you know, he would buck the system.

Laura: I'm also very much afraid for my children. They go to school in Boston and one of them lost his jacket, so I have good reason to be afraid.

Alex: Let me just say that I am a man and I'm still worried. I am. And even though I'm a man, usually you think a guy can protect himself or has at least an image of that. I still worry, because these kids today, you don't know if they're gonna pull a gun or a knife at age 13 or 12 or 14.

Geraldine: There's just so much of it.

Laura, Carol, Alex and Geraldine are not alone in their fear and concern. Public opinion polls in 1994 show that Americans consistently rate crime as one of the nation's most serious problems.[1] This book is about how crime is "constructed"—explained in terms of its causes and remedies—in the mass media and among regular people. It is based on a sample of newspaper commentary and on small group discussions involving more than 100 black and white residents of Boston, Massachusetts. The book's main purpose is to ascertain the significance of the prominent place crime occupies in American public life. Its secondary purpose is to advance our understanding of how people make sense of social problems.

THE CONSTRUCTIONIST PARADIGM

The book is situated within the constructionist paradigm for social problems research. Constructionist researchers tend to avoid questions about the objective nature of social problems (i.e., their sources, dimensions and possible remedies). Instead, they focus mostly on the political activities through which conditions—real or imagined—come to be viewed as problems in the first place. Of central concern in this line of inquiry has been the activities of "claimsmakers"—the politicians, grassroots activists, journalists and other social reformers who campaign to identify particular conditions as harmful and in need of amelioration. Best (1990), for example, examined the roles played by journalists and grass roots child advocates in drawing public attention to kidnapping, molestation, pornography and other threats to children. Reinarman and Levine (1989) similarly examined the roles played by Nancy Reagan, Republican and Democratic politicians and the Christian "New Right" in generating national concern about crack-cocaine.

Constructionist researchers also examine how problems come to be constructed or "framed" in particular ways. For example, Gusfield (1981) examined the cultural and political factors that contributed to the framing of "drinking-driving" as a problem stemming from morally defective individuals rather than public transportation policy or the design of automobiles. Gamson and Modigliani mapped out the rival frames on affirmative action (1987) and nuclear power (1989) and tracked their "careers" in samples of media discourse. And Gamson (1992) and Neuman, Just, and Crigler (1992) compared media frames with those expressed by ordinary people on issues in the news.

Constructionist investigations are clearly important to our understanding of the dynamics that govern public policy. What conditions come to be regarded as problems and how problems come to be framed in terms of causes and remedies necessarily influences legislation and the allocation of government resources. But the construction of social problems also affects a much wider range of phenomena. As Edelman (1988:12) puts it:

> Problems come into discourse and therefore into existence as reinforcements of ideologies, not simply because they are there or because they are important for wellbeing. They signify who are virtuous and useful and who are dangerous or inadequate, which actions will be rewarded and which penalized. They constitute people as subjects with particular kinds of aspirations, self-concepts, and fears, and they create beliefs about the relative importance of events and objects. They are critical in determining who exercise authority and who accept it. They construct areas of immunity from concern because those areas are not seen as problems.

Which conditions assume prominence as problems, and how those conditions are framed in terms of causes and remedies, thus influence not only public policy, but also the fates of politicians, interest groups, causes, and, ultimately, how Americans understand their social world.

THE CASE OF CRIME

There is an ongoing academic debate on the question of why Americans are so preoccupied with crime. Some argue that fear and concern of the sort expressed by Laura and her companions is a reasonable response to the extraordinary volume of crime in the United States. Currie (1985) points out, for example, that U.S. homicide rates are many times those of comparable industrial nations. And Wilson (1994) explains that the nature of violence in the U.S. is changing, that it is becoming more "random," and that offenders are younger than they used to be. Other analysts argue, however, that popular fear and concern are largely caused by media imagery and the rhetoric of enterprising politicians. Beckett (1994b) demonstrates, for example, that trends in popular concern about drugs match trends in sponsorship of the issue by political elites but not trends in actual drug abuse. Gerbner and Gross (1976) and Gerbner, Gross, Morgan, and Signorielli (1980) demonstrate that attentiveness to television correlates strongly with fear of crime.

But whatever the cause of popular fear and concern over crime, the issue's significance for politics and public policy depends on how it is constructed or framed. On this score there is a surprisingly robust conventional wisdom. Propounded by criminologists, sociologists and political analysts, the conventional wisdom goes like this: Americans, in the mass media and in everyday conversation, construct crime as a threat "from below" (Reiman, 1990). They view the typical offender as poor, male and usually black. They reject the notion that crime is caused by poverty or racial discrimination. Instead, they blame either individual moral failure or a poorly functioning criminal justice system. To solve the problem, they believe the police should crack down on offenders, and the courts should "get tough." Scheingold (1991) refers to this perspective as "volitional criminology." Gordon (1990), Dahrendorf (1985) and others call it a "law and order" orientation.[2]

POLITICS AND PUBLIC POLICY

Proponents of the conventional wisdom argue that attention to crime, because of the manner in which it tends to get framed, stimulates the expansion of the criminal justice system and the electoral success of conservative politicians.

Criminal Justice Expansion

The U.S. criminal justice system is growing dramatically by just about any measure. Chambliss (1994) reports that between 1972 and 1988 nationwide spending on criminal justice grew by 150 percent, and that between 1969 and 1989, per capita state expenditures on police and corrections increased tenfold. This spending financed a doubling in the size of the nation's police force between 1980 and 1990, and a massive expansion of the state and federal prison systems.

But prison building has hardly kept up with demand for cell space. Fueled by mandatory minimum sentences and restrictions on parole, especially for drug offenders, the nation's incarcerated population has skyrocketed. In the first six months of 1994 alone, the state and federal prison populations grew by 40,000, bringing the nation's total prison population to more than one million. If we add to this figure the one-day census of local jails, we arrive at a total incarcerated population of more than 1.4 million. The state and federal prison populations alone make for an incarceration *rate* (the number of prison inmates for every 100,000 U.S. residents) of 373, a nearly fourfold increase over the 1970 rate (*U.S. Department of Justice*, 1995; 1986). Indeed, in 1994 the United States boasted an incarceration rate five-to-eight times higher than most industrialized nations, and by far the highest rate of any record keeping nation except Russia (Mauer, 1994).

Other forms of corrections were also expanded in the last two decades. At one extreme, capital punishment was reinstated in 1977 and more than 250 inmates executed, including several that were minors when they committed their crimes, and others that were diagnosed as mentally retarded. At the opposite extreme, the ranks of probationers and parolees swelled to nearly 3.5 million; new forms of "community corrections," such as electronic monitoring and house arrest, gained popularity; and the number of Americans with criminal records on national databases grew into the tens of millions (Mauer, 1994; Gordon, 1990).

These developments have disproportionately affected minorities, especially African Americans. Nearly one in four African American men between the ages of 20 and 29 is now under the jurisdiction of the criminal justice system, either behind bars or on probation or parole. The proportions in some cities are even more striking; in Baltimore and Washington, D.C., between 40 and 50% of African American men between the ages of 18 and 35 are under criminal justice jurisdiction (Chambliss, 1994).

The "Violent Crime Control and Law Enforcement Act of 1994" (the "Crime Bill") will further accelerate the expansion of the criminal justice system. Passed by Congress and signed into law by President Clinton, the six-year, 30 billion dollar initiative provides for massive new prison construction and the hiring of 100,000 new police officers (for a 20% increase in the ranks of the nation's police). It also extends the death penalty to a range of new offenses, allows for the prosecution of 13 year olds as adults under certain circumstances, makes prison building grants to states contingent upon their compliance with a "truth in sentencing" provision, and includes the highly publicized "three strikes and you're out" rule that mandates life imprisonment for any individual convicted in federal court of a third serious felony or drug trafficking offense.

Analysts make two distinct arguments concerning the relationship between public opinion about crime and criminal justice expansion. One position holds that criminal justice expansion is evidence of well-functioning democracy (Wilson, 1983; Mayer, 1992). According to this view, popular concern about crime spurs politicians to act in the public interest by enlarging and toughening-up the justice system. The other position holds that popular law-and-order attitudes are a consequence of the speeches and campaigns of conservative politicians since Nixon (Beckett, 1994a; Chambliss, 1994). But this view, too, regards public opinion about crime as a driving force behind criminal justice expansion, albeit one that mediates rather than causes elite political action.

Conservative Political Success

Republicans held the United States' highest political office during 20 of the 24 years between 1968 and 1992. Massive Republican electoral gains during the 1994 mid-term elections suggest that Democrat Bill Clinton's 1992 Presidential victory was more an aberration than an indication of fundamental change. Proponents of the conventional wisdom argue that Republican dominance over national politics is fueled, in part, by the politics of crime. Beckett (1994a), for example, catalogues the list of conservatives—Richard Nixon, Barry Goldwater, George Wallace, Spiro Agnew, Ronald Reagan, and George Bush among them— who campaigned on "law and order" platforms, and when elected, waged wars on drugs and crime. Gordon (1990) points to the "Willie Horton" advertisements run by the 1988 Bush Campaign. Horton was the convicted murderer who escaped from a Massachusetts prison furlough program while Democratic presidential nominee Michael Dukakis was governor. While at-large, Horton raped a Maryland woman and stabbed her fiancee. The Bush campaign ads featured the black man's face while a voice-over made the apparently devastating point: The Democrat who would be president is *soft on crime.*

Why is crime, as a political issue, so beneficial to conservatives? Proponents of the conventional wisdom make four arguments. First, like the cold war, crime supplies conservatives with an enemy against whom they can rally middle Americans in a common struggle. This is especially valuable to Republican politicians whose economic policies favor the rich (Scheingold, 1984, 1991; Reiman, 1990). Second, crime benefits conservatives because its presence on the public agenda crowds out issues, such as poverty, health care and education, that imply a need for income redistribution or governmental initiative (Edelman, 1988; Scheingold, 1991). Third, because white Americans tend to conflate criminality with blackness, Republican politicians are able to successfully use the issue of crime to drive a wedge through the Democratic Party's inter-racial coalition (Edsall, 1991; Gordon, 1990; Beckett, 1994a). Finally, if the conventional wisdom is correct with respect to public opinion, then from a strictly ideological standpoint, conservatives are closer than liberals to the views of most Americans on crime and its remedies (Jencks, 1992).

EMPIRICAL EVIDENCE

But is the conventional wisdom on how Americans construct crime correct? There is, of course, a good deal of prima-facie evidence that says "yes." We know, for example, that Americans tend to attribute responsibility for all manner of behavior to individuals rather than societal forces (Gans, 1988). And among the most robust findings of public opinion polling is that Americans increasingly favor capital punishment and view the courts as too lenient (Komarnicki and Doble, 1986; Mayer, 1992; Niemi, Mueller and Smith, 1989). But when we go beyond these general observations to look at what the best academic studies reveal, the picture becomes more complicated.

Public Opinion

Among the most commonly cited scholarly studies of public thinking about crime are *Crime and Punishment: Changing Attitudes in America,* by Arthur Stinchcombe and his colleagues (1980), and *Crime News and the Public,* by Doris Graber (1980). Both are already a bit dated, and both provide only mixed support for the conventional account.

The authors of *Crime and Punishment* examined responses over many years to questions in the General Social Survey on fear of crime, capital punishment, the courts and gun control. They demonstrate that during the 1960s and 1970s, while the public was expressing increasingly liberal attitudes on issues such as abortion, feminism and race relations, it was growing more punitive on the issue of crime. To resolve this paradox, they examined cross-sectional survey data on opinions on a variety of political issues. They conclude that the relationship between "liberalism" and "lenience" is weak, the result of perhaps one percent of the population ("extreme liberals") for whom liberal values extend to criminal justice practices. For the vast majority, the "law and order" response to crime is common sense. Thus, *Crime and Punishment* seems to support the conventional wisdom described in the first part of this chapter. But against the notion that the issue is settled, the authors readily admit that the data upon which they base their conclusions is "thin." In their words,

> [E]ven though popular criminology is replete with theories on what kinds of people commit crimes, we have no questions on what makes for a criminal character and what should be done about it. . . . [O]ur poll questions on attitudes toward crime and punishment tap only a few aspects of the public's overall views about the causes and control of crime. (pp. 5–6)

Doris Graber's study examined the influence of news reports about crime on public thinking. Her research team analyzed all of the crime stories appearing in the course of one year in a large sample of media sources, and contrasted their content with findings from interview research. The interviews, conducted at regular intervals throughout the same year, involved three panels, each comprised of 48 respondents. We will note Graber's findings on media discourse in the following section; here we are concerned with what she learned from her interview respondents. In support of the conventional wisdom, Graber discovered that her respondents viewed the crime threat as principally emanating from poor people, especially the minority poor. Moreover, when asked to name the most important causes of crime, they placed the "bulk of the blame" (49% of attributions) on "personal factors" such as peer pressure, greed, and deficiencies in home life. But against the conventional wisdom, Graber reports that more than one-third (34.6%) of her panelists' attributions for crime were to poverty, economic stress and unemployment (p. 72). She concludes that most panelists saw "social conditions, particularly poverty and poor home life, as the primary causes of crime, thus absolving individual criminals and their ethnic groups, at least in part" (p. 127). Thus, Graber's study is best regarded as ambivalent in its bearing on the conventional wisdom.[3]

In the absence of more up-to-date scholarly research on public opinion about crime, writers have turned to the publications of the large polling agencies such as Gallup, Ropers and Harris (e.g., Gordon, 1990; Scheingold, 1991). But the publications of these organizations tend to raise as many questions as they answer. To illustrate the problem, let me describe some of the conclusions of a 1989 Gallup Report entitled "Frustrated by Criminal Justice System, Public Demands Harsher Penalties." The Gallup writers provide ample support for their conclusion that the public increasingly has a "get tough attitude toward law enforcement." Specifically, they report that 83% of Americans believe that the "court's treatment of criminals" is "not harsh enough," and that "drugs" has replaced "unemployment" as the single factor held to be most responsible for crime.[4] But in the same report they note that Americans, by a two-to-one margin, believe that the most effective way to fight crime is to "attack social problems" rather than to "improve law enforcement."[5] These findings are inconsistent. If in fact the public exhibits a "law and order" attitude, then why by such a large margin does it prefer anticrime measures that focus on the "social and economic problems that lead to crime"? Of course, it is possible to interpret the poll data in such a way as to conjure a coherent picture of public opinion. But taken on their own terms, they can hardly be offered as either definitive support for, or refutation of, the conventional wisdom on public opinion about crime.[6]

Media Discourse

The evidence concerning mass media constructions of crime is similarly mixed. Beckett (1994a) examined newspaper commentary and

newsmagazine discourse on crime between 1965 and 1973. She argues
that the dominant media frame during this period attributes crime to
permissiveness and the "mollycodlling" of criminals. Elias (1993) examined all of the crime stories and attending photographs appearing in the
newsweeklies *Time, U.S. News and World Report,* and *Newsweek* between
1956 and 1991. Also in support of the conventional wisdom, he argues
that the newsweeklies attribute crime to "evil people," depict the typical
offender as black, and call for tougher penalties, "endless resources" for
law enforcement, and the easing of legal restraints on police conduct.
But analysts of media discourse are by no means unanimous. In the
study described above, for example, Graber finds no support for the
notion that the media depicts criminals as "flawed in character, nonwhite
and lower class." In contrast to Elias and Beckett, she finds that "crime
and justice news . . . represents a medley of conflicting views and
motivations."[7]

* * * * *

The scholarly record is thus a weak basis for drawing the conclusion
that Americans construct crime in a "law and order" fashion, and thus
similarly for the conclusion that media and popular constructions of
crime are a force behind criminal justice expansion and the electoral
success of conservative politicians. The prima-facie evidence in support
of the conventional wisdom, however, remains compelling. This book
puts the conventional wisdom to the test. In the following chapter, I
explain in greater detail why opinion polling of the sort practiced by
Gallup and other polling firms has failed to live up to its promise and
describe the details of my alternative approach. But before proceeding, I
would like to set down some of the latter's basic premises.

FRAME ANALYSIS

The research strategy adopted for this study builds on the work of
Gamson (1988, 1992), Gamson and Modigliani (1989, 1987), Neuman et
al. (1992) and Beckett (1994a). Known as "frame analysis," the strategy is
best regarded as a methodology for conducting research in the constructionist paradigm. It rests on three basic premises.

1. People should be regarded as active assemblers of meaning. In
constructing accounts of public issues, they draw upon the resources at
their disposal including popular wisdom, their personal experiences,
and bits of media discourse. To assemble this raw material into coherent

and meaningful accounts, they select from the range of interpretive frameworks available in the culture for making meaning on the issue at hand (cf. Miller and Holstein, 1993).[8]

Gamson, Croteau, Hoynes, and Sasson (1992:384) point out that the concept of interpretive framework derives strength from its ambivalence on the question of structure versus agency.

> On the one hand, events and experiences are framed; on the other hand, we frame events and experiences. Goffman warns us that "organizational premises are involved, and those are something cognition arrives at, not something cognition creates or generates." At the same time, he calls attention to the fragility of frames in use and their vulnerability to tampering. This underlines the usefulness of framing as a bridging concept between cognition and culture. A cultural level analysis tells us that our political world is framed, that reported events are pre-organized and do not come to us in raw form. But we are active processors and however encoded our received reality, we may decode it in different ways.

Frames on public problems typically feature a diagnostic component that identifies a condition as intolerable and attributes blame or causality, and a prognostic component that prescribes one or more courses of ameliorative action (cf. Snow and Benford, 1988; Gusfield, 1981). Frames can be evoked through catch-phrases, historical exemplars, public figures and other types of condensing symbols (Gamson 1988). Finally, frames tend to have more or less standard rebuttals.

2.   The creation of meaning through the work of framing occurs in various forums, including academic journals, the mass media, and everyday conversation (cf. Ibarra and Kitsuse, 1993). These ought best be treated as discrete cultural systems each with its own norms and vocabularies and each deserving of study in its own right. No a priori judgments should be made about how the various forums relate one to the other. Because the mass media is presently the principal venue for public discourse, I will use the terms "media discourse" and "public discourse" interchangeably. I will use the term "popular discourse" to refer to what Neuman et al. (1992:141) term "common language" and the "natural discourse of the mass public."

3.   Political conflicts on particular issues are fought out as symbolic contests between contesting frames. Politicians, grass roots activists, journalists and other claimsmakers vie with one another to get their preferred frames before the public and to rebut those of their rivals. They measure their own success in this venture by the degree of visibility they win for their preferred frames (Gamson et al., 1992).

The emphasis in frame analytic research on public opinion and media discourse has been, for the most part, on describing the contours and dynamics of frame contests (Gamson and Modigliani, 1989; Gamson, 1992; Beckett, 1994a); the relationships between public and popular discourse (Gamson, 1992; Neuman et al., 1992); and the manner in which ordinary people construct meaning (Gamson, 1992). This book pursues each of these lines of inquiry. Specifically, I answer five questions: (1) What are the contesting frames on crime? (2) Which frames are dominant in the public discourse? (3) Which are dominant in popular discourse? (4) Why are some frames more successful than others? (5) What (therefore) is the significance of the prominent place crime occupies in American public life?

WHAT FOLLOWS

The architecture of the book is straightforward. Chapter 2 identifies the crime frames and discusses the study's discourse samples and methodology. Next, Chapters 3–6 describe the frames' "performances" in the samples of public and popular discourse. Chapters 7 and 8 then develop a constructionist theoretical explanation for why certain frames performed well while others did not. Finally, Chapter 9 presents the book's conclusions.

NOTES

1. See, for example, the *Time Magazine* cover story, "Lock 'Em Up," Feburary 7, 1994.
2. Among the many analysts who contribute to the conventional wisdom: Dahrendorf, 1985; Edsall, 1991; Elias, 1993; Gordon, 1990; Jencks, 1992; Johns, 1992; Scheingold, 1991, 1984; Quinney, 1974, 1970; Reiman, 1990; Rubin, 1988.
3. Roberts' (1992:131) comprehensive review of scholarly studies of public opinion on the causes of crime and arrived at a similarly ambivalent conclusion: "[T]here is no single cause of crime identified by a majority of the American public. The public appears to adopt a multi-dimensional view of the origin of crime."
4. In 1981, and again in 1989, respondents were asked the open ended question "In your opinion, what factors are most responsible for crime in the U.S. today?" In 1981, 37% of respondents' attributions for crime were to "unemployment" and 13% were to "drugs." In 1989, 58% of respondents' attributions were to "drugs" and only 14% to unemployment.

5.   In response to the following statement, 61% of respondents selected "attack social problems" and 32% selected "improve law enforcement": "To lower the crime rate in the U.S., some people think additional money and effort should go to attacking the social and economic
problems that lead to crime, through better education and job training.
Others feel more money and effort should go to deterring crime by
improving law enforcement with more prisons, police and judges. Which
comes closer to your view?"

6.   Another inconsistency from the same publication: In 1981, the
year that 37% of respondents' attributions for crime were to unemployment, 38% favored "harsher punishment" as a crime reduction strategy.
But by 1989, after the public had reportedly become more punitive, the
proportion of respondents favoring "harsher punishment" dropped to
24%! Based on this observation, one might conclude that the public has
grown *less* punitive. But the real point is not that the Gallup staff misin-
terpreted its survey; rather, it is that Gallup surveys, and others, can be
interpreted in different ways.

7.   For a review of other studies of mass media constructions of
crime, see Bortner, 1984 and Roberts, 1992. The most elaborate research on this topic has been done outside the United States. On the
British media, see Hall, Critcher, Jefferson, Clarke, and Roberts, 1978
and Cohen and Young, 1981. On the Canadian media, see Ericson,
Baranek, and Chan, 1991.

8.   The concept of interpretive framework or "frame" comes from
Goffman, 1974. Its application to the field of political sociology is devel-
oped in Tuchman, 1978; Gitlin, 1980; Snow, Rochford, Worden, and
Benford, 1986; Snow and Benford, 1988; Gamson, 1988; Gamson and
Modigliani, 1987, 1989; and Gamson et al., 1992.

2

PRELIMINARIES

This book's method is to track the performances of a handful of culturally available frames on street crime in samples of media and popular discourse. This chapter is intended to lay the foundation for what follows by identifying the frames and describing the samples of discourse.

THE CONTESTING FRAMES

In order to establish a catalogue of culturally available frames on street crime, I examined the speeches and publications of partisans on various "sides" of the issue.[1] There are two advantages to this strategy: First, frame sponsors tend to express their views in an ideologically coherent manner, thus presenting relatively "pure" or unadulterated frames. Second, by first consulting sponsors rather than mass media products, I could create a catalogue that comes close to including all culturally available frames rather than only those that enjoy prominence in the mass media.

My review of the activist and partisan discourse yielded a working catalogue of frames. I then tested the "fit" of this catalogue on the sample of media discourse assembled for the study. My aim at this stage was to make sure that the frame catalogue offered the right balance between precision (it should represent all of the important views and ideas in the crime debate) and economy (it should summarize and simplify the debate). The final, revised catalogue included five basic frames that I labeled *Faulty System, Blocked Opportunities, Social Breakdown, Media Violence* and *Racist System*. They are presented in the coding guide (Appendix B) in terms of their constituent elements. In what follows I describe them as ideal types.

Faulty System

The "law and order" perspective described in the introduction is best captured in the frame *Faulty System*. This frame regards crime as a consequence of impunity: People do crimes because they know they can get away with them. The police are handcuffed by liberal judges. The prisons, bursting at their seams, have revolving doors for serious offenders. "The system is riddled with loopholes and technicalities that render punishment neither swift nor certain," says Bush Administration Attorney General William P. Barr (P.A.F., 1993:13). "The Supreme Court of our country has made it almost impossible to convict a criminal," says Alabama governor George Wallace (Gordon, 1990:176). The only way to enhance public safety is to increase the swiftness, certainty and severity of punishment. In the words of President Richard M. Nixon, "The time has come for soft-headed judges and probation officers to show as much concern for the rights of innocent victims of crime as they do for the rights of convicted criminals" (1973:355). Loopholes and technicalities that impede the apprehension and imprisonment of offenders must be eliminated. Adequate funding for police, courts and prisons must be made available. In our failure to act, warns political scientist James Q. Wilson, "We thereby trifle with the wicked, make sport of the innocent, and encourage the calculating" (P.A.F., 1993:15).

Faulty System is sponsored by Republican politicians, conservative policy analysts, and most criminal justice professionals. It can be symbolically condensed with the mug-shot of the convicted rapist Willie Horton, or by the image of inmates passing through a revolving door on a prison gate (both symbols courtesy of commercials aired on behalf of George Bush in the 1988 presidential campaign [see Chapter 1]).

Blocked Opportunities

The frame *Blocked Opportunities* depicts crime as a consequence of inequality and discrimination, especially as they manifest themselves in unemployment, poverty, and inadequate educational opportunities. People commit crimes when they discover that the legitimate means for attaining material success are blocked. In the words of President Lyndon B. Johnson, "Unemployment, ignorance, disease, filth, poor housing, congestion, discrimination—all of these things contribute to the great crime wave that is sweeping through our nation" (Beckett, 1994a). The United States is unique among industrialized societies in both the extent of its income inequality and the weakness of its social safety net. Moreover, since the 1960s the deindustrialization of American cities and attendant disappearance of good paying blue-collar jobs has steadily worsened prospects for the urban poor. Growing desperation promotes violence as well as property crime; in the words of criminologist David Bruck, "If you're going to create a sink-or-swim society, you have to expect people to thrash before they go down" (P.A.F., 1993:22). To reduce crime, government must ameliorate the social conditions that cause it. In the words of former Minneapolis Police Chief Anthony Bouza, "Only the government can provide an educational plan that serves the poor, a welfare system that attends to the needs of the excluded and jobs programs that offer hope to all our citizens. . . . The War on Poverty must be refought. The dilemma of racism must be attacked" (Bouza, 1993:20).

Blocked Opportunities is sponsored by liberal and Left policy analysts and by some liberal Democrat politicians. It can be symbolically condensed through references to the dead-end jobs reserved for inner-city youth, such as "flipping burgers at McDonalds."

Social Breakdown

The frame *Social Breakdown* depicts crime as a consequence of family and community disintegration. Witness the skyrocketing rates of divorce and out-of-wedlock births. Witness the indifference of urbanites to the crime that plagues their communities. Family breakdown in the context of urban indifference has loosened the moral and social bonds that in better times discouraged crime. As President Clinton explained in his 1994 State of the Union message, "In America's toughest neighborhoods, meanest streets, and poorest rural areas, we have seen a stunning breakdown of community, family and work—the heart and soul of civilized society. This has created a vast vacuum into which violence, drugs and gangs have moved." The remedy for the problem can be found in collective efforts to reconstitute family and community through moral exhortation, neighborhood associations, crime watches and community policing. "Every parent, every teacher, every person who has the chance to influence children must force a change in the lives of our kids," urged the President in his weekly radio address. "We have to show them we love them, and we have to teach them discipline and responsibility." The frame can be symbolically condensed through laments over the decline of "family values" and by the figure of Kitty Genovese, the New York woman who was stabbed to death while her neighbors looked passively on (see Chapter 4).

Social Breakdown is typically expressed in a neutral, ostensibly non-ideological fashion, but the frame also has conservative and liberal versions. The conservative versions attributes family and community breakdown to "permissiveness," the protest movements of the 1960s and 70s (e.g., civil rights, feminism) and government-sponsored antipoverty initiatives (e.g., "welfare"). As Senator Daniel Patrick Moynihan put it,

"Among a large and growing lower class, self-reliance, self discipline and industry are waning . . . [F]amilies are more and more matrifocal and atomized; crime and disorder are sharply on the rise. . . . It is a stirring, if generally unrecognized, demonstration of the power of the welfare machine" (Beckett, 1994a). The liberal versions, in contrast, attribute family and community breakdown to unemployment, racial discrimination, deindustrialization and capital flight.

Media Violence

The frame *Media Violence* depicts crime as a consequence of violence on television, in the movies and in popular music. Violence in the mass media undermines respect for life. By the time the average child reaches age 18, notes Dr. Thomas Elmendorf in testimony before the House Subcommittee on Communication, "he will have witnessed . . . some 18,000 murders and countless highly detailed incidents of robbery, arson, bombings, shooting, beatings, forgery, smuggling and torture." As a result, "Television has become a school of violence and a college for crime" (1976:764). To reduce violence in the society we must first reduce it in the mass media.

Media Violence can be symbolically condensed through reference to violent television programs (e.g., *Miami Vice*) or musicians whose lyrics are said to promote violence (e.g., "Guns 'N' Roses," "2 Live Crew"). The frame is sponsored by citizen lobby organizations (e.g., the Massachusetts based group Action for Children's Television), and, periodically, by members of Congress and the Department of Justice.

Racist System

The fifth frame, *Racist System,* derives its essence from a depiction of the criminal justice system rather than an attribution of responsibility for crime. The frame depicts the courts and police as racist agents of oppression. In the words of Johnson Administration Undersecretary of State Nicholas deB. Katzenbach, "We have in these United States lived under a dual system of justice, one for the white, one for the black" (1968:616). Police resources are dedicated to the protection of low crime white neighborhoods rather than high crime minority ghettos. Black offenders are more likely to be arrested, convicted and sentenced to prison than whites who commit comparable offenses. And the death penalty is administered in a racist fashion. In some versions of this frame, the putative purpose of the criminal justice system is to suppress a potentially rebellious underclass.

Racist System is sponsored by civil rights and civil liberties activists and by Left intellectuals. It can be condensed by reference to Rodney King or other well-known targets of racially motivated police violence.

Rebuttals

Each of these five frames has a number of standard rebuttals. *Faulty System*, for example, is frequently negated with the claim that imprisonment "hardens" offenders; *Blocked Opportunities* with the claim that most poor people are straight as an arrow; *Social Breakdown* with the claim that rhetoric about the "nuclear family" is in fact thinly veiled hostility for feminism; and so on. The coding guide (Appendix B) specifies some of the frames' most common negations. Table 2.1 illustrates the frames' key components.

There is one more matter to clarify concerning my catalogue of frames. In contemporary discourse, crime is often attributed to drugs and guns. I made an early decision that drugs and guns are part of the crime problem—things that demand explanation and not explanations in themselves. If in the account that follows "drugs" and "guns" are conspicuously absent as a "causes" of crime, it is for this reason.

MEDIA DISCOURSE

The sample of media discourse created for this study is comprised of 58 op ed columns on the topic of street crime. The op eds appeared in six metropolitan newspapers during a twelve month period between 1990 and 1991. The newspapers include the *New York Times*, the *Washington Post*, the *Chicago Tribune*, the *Boston Globe*, the *Atlanta Constitution*, and the *Los Angeles Times*. Items were initially included in the sample if they addressed the topic of street crime and appeared opposite the editorial page or in the expanded commentary section of the Sunday paper. The sample was subsequently winnowed to include only items that displayed at least one of the crime frames either for the purpose of advocacy or rebuttal. Of the handful of op eds excluded at this stage of data compilation, most were pieces that merely described the seriousness of the crime problem without offering either an analysis of its sources or recommendation for its cure.

The sample is representative of one type of media discourse: that of public policy commentary by political, journalistic and academic elites. In contrast to entertainment programming (e.g., police dramas) op eds tend to be explicit in their ideological messages. In contrast to staight

Table 2.1. Crime Frames

	Diagnosis	Prognosis	Condensing Symbols
Faulty System	Crime stems from criminal justice leniency and inefficiency	The criminal justice system needs to "get tough."	Willie Horton "Handcuffed police" "Revolving door justice"
Blocked Opportunities	Crime stems from poverty and inequality	The government must address the "root causes" of crime by creating jobs and reducing poverty.	"Flipping Burgers" at McDonalds
Social Breakdown	Crime stems from family and community breakdown.	Citizens should band together to recreate traditional communities.	"Take back the streets" Kitty Genovese "Family values"
Media Violence	Crime stems from violence in the mass media	The government should regulate violent imagery in the media.	"Life imitates art" 2 Live Crew Guns n Roses
Racist System	The criminal justice system operates in a racist fashion.	African Americans should band together to demand justice.	Rodney King Crown Heights Charles Stuart

news reporting, op eds, when taken as a whole, tend to be ideologically diverse. Beckett (1995) attributes this diversity to the relative autonomy of op ed writers from official (governmental and law enforcement) sources. Gans (1979) points out that newspaper editors feel compelled by a professional "balance norm" to publish roughly equal numbers of expressly conservative and liberal columns. While distinct in these respect from other types of media discourse, op eds feature the key tropes and metaphors that punctuate the public debate on crime. They are also significant for their effects on public policy; politicians read op eds to get a sense of where the political winds are blowing and thereby to arrive at conclusions about what to say and do.

POPULAR DISCOURSE

The shortcomings of survey research for gathering data on public opinion are widely recognized: Surveys tend to produce findings that reflect the concepts and categories of their authors rather than their subjects (Reinharz, 1984); they treat opinions as stable when in fact opinions vary with context (Potter and Wetherell, 1987; Bennett, 1980); and they foster an image of people as isolated individuals rather than members of particular cultures and subcultures (Blumer, 1948). At the root of the problem is that survey research rests on a faulty depiction of the research subject: It assumes that each person carries about in her head a fixed and relatively simple structure of attitudes. But in the real world, human consciousness is bound up with social context and language, both rife with shades of symbolic meaning. What people think and say depends in part on who is asking, who is listening, how the question is posed, and a host of related details. Surveys, in spite of the best efforts of skilled researchers, cannot adequately deal with this complexity.

Michael Billig's (1987, 1991) depiction of the research subject is perhaps the alternative most compatible with the constructionist approach to public opinion. He contends that thinking is nothing more than a dialogue or an argument occurring in a single self. Hence public conversation and private thinking can be treated analytically as part and parcel of the same process. The best way to analyze both is to regard people as orators and to examine the rhetorical components of their arguments. Prominent among the latter are "common-places"—the contrary themes, maxims, folk wisdom, values, and so forth, that together comprise a culture's common sense. But how can we sample the work of everyday orators?

Peer Group Discussions

Peer group discussions (Gamson, 1992) are ideally suited to producing discourse for the kind of analysis Billig proposes. Like the conventional focus group (Morgan, 1988), of which they are a variation, they permit the researcher to listen in as subjects use their own categories and vocabularies to cooperatively create meaning. But unlike conventional focus groups, the participants in the peer group are acquainted with one another *outside* of the research setting. This difference offers two advantages: First, peer group participants typically interact with greater intensity and less reserve than their focus group counterparts. This, in turn, permits the facilitator to minimize his or her involvement in the discussion and results in richer transcripts. Second, because the peer groups have a social existence independent of the sociologist's contrivance, their discourse can be regarded with greater confidence as reflective of the particular subcultures from which they are drawn.

Recruitment

I decided to constitute peer groups from a sample of neighborhood crime watch groups because the latter are venues in which urbanites regularly meet to talk about crime (Appendix C describes what crime watch groups do other than create discourse for sociological research). Working from a list provided by the crime watch division of the Boston Police Department, I contacted group organizers by mail and telephone and asked them to host a discussion with four to six members of their group. To achieve a racial balance in group type I recruited both from communities of color and neighborhoods that are mostly white. In all, I contacted about 60 organizers and arranged 20 successful interviews (I also conducted several pilot sessions to rehearse the format). My effort to achieve racial balance proved successful: Of the twenty interview groups, eight were white, nine black, and three mixed.[2]

The groups were from the working and middle class residential areas of seven Boston neighborhoods. The black groups were from Roxbury, Mattapan, and parts of Dorchester, all segregated black communities. The white groups were from Jamaica Plain, South End, Roslindale and Mission Hill, predominantly white communities but among the most integrated in the city.[3] Six of the seven neighborhoods have housing stocks that consist mostly of single and two-family dwellings with an occasional apartment building or public housing development.[4] Though there are crime watch groups in the latter, none are included in this sample.

These neighborhoods have in common their close proximity to what Wilson (1987) describes as "underclass" zones. The frontier dividing the shady streets and well kept houses of the former from the vacant lots and boarded up buildings of the latter is sometimes as narrow as a single street. This is especially true for several of the black groups. But even in these cases the distinction between the two areas is real enough.

Boston neighborhoods endure a great deal of crime, a fact that becomes especially apparent when we compare the rates of street crime offenses within the city with those statewide. The city comprises less than 10% of Massachusetts's population, but approximately one third of all homicides statewide, one fourth of all rapes, and nearly one half of all robberies, occur within the city (U.S. Department of Justice, 1992). Notably, however, while most city neighborhoods suffer crime rates that are higher than those statewide, the aggregate figures reported here mask the disproportionate concentration of street crime in Boston's minority neighborhoods. In 1990, for example, 81% of all homicides, 54% of all rapes and 46% of all robberies occurred in Roxbury, Dorchester and Mattapan, the three neighborhoods from which all of the black groups participating in this study were drawn (Boston Police Department, 1992).

The Discussions

The discussions were structured around six questions aimed at generating discourse on the dimensions of the crime problem, its sources, and its most promising remedies. They were run by a facilitator whose race matched that of the group members. Matching the race of the facilitator and group members was important because doing so minimized the influence that norms of politeness—or against the airing of "dirty laundry"—might otherwise have had on the discussions. The first pilot discussion was conducted in the Fall of 1991; the final discussion was in the Winter of 1993.

The interview schedule (Appendix A) was designed with two goals in mind: First, I wanted to ensure that the conversationalists would have ample opportunity to come up with their own shared frames on crime. Second, I wanted to be sure to get their reactions to the frames that are the subject of this study. Accordingly, the schedule began with two general questions aimed at sparking open conversation on the dimensions and sources of the crime problem. These questions were followed by a series of three statements, one representing each of the first three frames described above. The conversationalists were asked to state whether they agreed or disagreed with each of the statements, and to explain their viewpoints.

The frame *Racist System* was not prompted with a statement; instead, reaction to it was elicited separately through a question about a highly publicized murder investigation that occassioned public discourse on police violations of civil rights. I decided to trigger *Racist System* using this *indirect* approach because of the highly charged nature of its claims. As things turn out, the strategy proved only partially successful in averting a breakdown of rapport between the facilitator and the group. The full story is told in Chapter 6.

In contrast to the other frames, *Media Violence* was not prompted in any fashion whatsoever. Where it emerged in the discussions it did so spontaneously. In fact, it was only after examining the discussion transcripts that I decided to code for the presence of the frame.

The facilitators did not participate in the discussions in any way, beyond asking the interview questions. Upon arrival at each session, they explained to the participants that they would be audiotaping the discussion and taking notes in order to keep track of who was speaking. After asking each question, they broke off eye contact by attending to the task of note-taking. The conversationalists were thus, in effect, left to negotiate their own response to each question.

Typicality of the Sample

Who participated in the discussions? To what population can we generalize from this sample? In all, 110 Boston residents participated in the peer group discussions. The profile that follows is based on information provided by the participants in a brief questionnaire filled out at the conclusion of each session. The sample population is more racially balanced than the larger population of Boston (50% of the participants are white, 47% African American) but underrepresents Hispanic and Asian Americans (less than 3% of the sample). It is also more female (71%) and a bit better educated than the larger population (40% finished college).[5] With respect to age, it is right on target for people 60 and older (21%), but overrepresents people in the 40–59 bracket at the expense of younger residents (42 and 26% of the sample, respectively).[6]

The most intuitively significant characteristic of the sample is that it is comprised of participants in crime watch groups. But for three reasons, this turns out to be less important than at first it might seem. First, the participants in this study are not anticrime zealots. For most, crime watch membership involves no more than attending meetings in a neighbor's living room a few times each year. Second, while the participants are certainly fearful of crime, survey research (Stinchcombe et al., 1980; Cullen, Clark, Cullen, and Mathers, 1985) has failed to identify any relationship between this variable and attitudes about crime's causes and remedies. Third, research has also failed to sustain the common sense notion that people who participate in crime watch are either unusually fearful or unusually punitive. After reviewing the best studies in this area, Lewis and Salem (1986:129) conclude that "there is no systematic evidence that an individual's attitude toward crime is associated with participation in collective responses."

Thus, with respect to the issue of generalizability, the fact that the participants attend crime watch meetings is likely a red herring. But there is no getting around the limitations associated with my choice of a qualitative research strategy. In general, qualitative techniques afford greater accuracy with respect to a given sample population ("internal validity"), but they do so at the cost of precision when generalizing to some larger population ("external validity"). This tradeoff is somewhat less troubling when studying consciousness about crime than when attempting to predict the outcome of a closely contested election (cf. Roberts, 1992). Nevertheless, the relatively small and nonrandom nature of the study sample means that we ought not use it as a basis for making claims about Americans as a whole.

Who, then, do the study participants represent? A reasonable supposition is that they are typical of their neighbors and the kinds of people who live in neighborhoods of the same type. For whites, this means urban neighborhoods that are racially integrated (if primarily white) and that adjoin high crime "underclass" areas. For blacks, this means the nicer streets and blocks in segregated minority communities. (I will take up the question of how such people compare to Americans as a whole in the concluding chapter).

There is one final point to be made concerning the study sample and design. The peer group technique is itself a device for minimizing the kind of sample bias that bedevils qualitative researchers who use more conventional interviewing techniques. Because the discussion created by the group is a collective product, it tends to reflect the common sense of the subculture from which its participants are drawn. Indeed, as Gamson points out (1992:192), meaningful interaction within a group is only possible to the extent that its members share taken-for-granted assumptions about the world—*intersubjectivity*, in Schutz's (1967) term. Group interaction dynamics thus tend to discourage the expression of marginal ideas, encouraging instead ideas that are in broad currency within a particular subculture. This tends to be the case regardless of the precise composition of the group. While the presence of a few "outliers" (individuals with idiosyncratic views) can badly skew the results of conventional interview research, their presence within a peer group tends not to pose so much of a problem.

Fear of Crime

Most of this book describes how people *explain* crime. But what is the nature of the problem that demands explanation? What, in other words, are the peer group discussion participants afraid of? The first interview question asked "What crimes are you most concerned about and who is doing them?" The participants answered, for the most part, that they are fearful of "bodily harm" and not merely of losing "material things." Burglaries and car thefts are a hassle and a "violation," but they pale in significance in comparison to "drive-by shootings" and "random acts of violence." The following excerpts, from an African American and a white participant, respectively, are typical:

Group: Troy Street

Vanessa: To me the most scariest aspect of crime is really not the property issue . . . I don't have a great attachment to my car or anything in my house necessarily. It's just a piece of thing that—you know—I'll make a claim, I'll get the money and I'll replace it . . . I worry more about, you know, just walking down the street one day and being in the way of a random shootings.

Group: Dean Avenue

Carolyn: I think I'm afraid of the personal violence—of being attacked . . . I've been robbed two or three times. You can survive that, I mean material things don't matter.

Who is committing these crimes? The conversationalists insisted that crime is committed by all types of people in all types of neighborhoods, thus implicitly repudiating the stereotype of the black male offender (see Chapter 1). But at the same time they discussed which neighborhoods and bus routes ought best be avoided in the interests of safety, thus revealing "cognitive maps" that accurately reflect the actual distribution of violent street crime in the city.[7] The following excerpts are, once again, from an African American and a white speaker, respectively:

Group: Pleasant Street

Libby: Like when I told my friend, well I live on Walker Street but I take the bus and get off on Plymouth Street side. I do not come Parker way side . . . I'll tell them in a minute, "If you come to my house don't come Parker way. Don't get on the

11 to come to my house. Take the 33—" *In a minute.* I tell them get on the 33. Do *not* get on the Parker. No telling who's out on the corner.

Group: Jacob's Lane

Geraldine: I came originally from Dorchester and now it's sad—I mean, I never thought this day would come. But we really don't, if we can possible help it, go down through Cummins Highway and Mattapan. And that's where I was brought up.

In discussing their fears, the conversationalists referred to first hand experiences of victimization as well as to news stories about crime happenings. But the large volume of references to the former can be read as a challenge to the claim that fear of crime among urbanites is in some sense irrational, stemming from either media hype (see Gerbner et al., 1980; Gerbner and Gross, 1976), or "incivility" and other signs of neighborhood decay (see Lewis and Salem, 1986; Skogan, 1990). For example, consider the following exchange between members of one black group:

Group: Fisher Hill Road
Cast:

Chuck, a printing estimator and high school graduate, in his early 40s.
Deborah, a facilities manager and high school graduate, in her late 30s.
Georgia, a director of administrative services and high school graduate, in her late 30s.
Karl, a research and development aid and high school graduate, in his mid 50s.
Victor, retired, in his mid 60s.
Sam, retired, in his 70s.

Chuck: I tell you a real big problem is, ah, we can say that I found two loaded pistols on my property. These guys— And I just found handguns. There have been shotguns found, you name it—
Deborah: Automatic weapons.
Chuck: —pump shotguns and stuff like that. And they just put them anywhere. They could be in a bag, and they'll just lay it down. And it looks like its just a piece of trash but there's a gun in it. Laying out anywheres. Any kid on the street could pick it up . . .
Gloria: And also one of the children have found packages of

crack that one of the drug dealers had dropped because the police were coming. And they ingested it. It was very fortunate that the mother knew exactly what to do or that child probably would have been dead . . .

Deborah: As I was saying, the unprovoked violence is a problem too in that—There's a school yard not far from here, and they just stand out there at any time of the day or night and shoot. And a lot of kids are out there playing basketball, football, what have you. Innocent kids who could have some harm come to them as a result of these idiots.

Karl: Some *have had* some harm. You all got to remember we had a little girl shot right on the head because another drug dealer was shooting at another drug dealer. A little small child.

Gloria: And I don't think I'm wrong in saying that just about every house on this street and River Street have had shots fired into their homes or at their homes.

Victor: I know—Well, I had the windshield shot out.

Karl: I know, I don't know about the them next to you, but the next two down and mine, I've seen bullet holes.

Gloria: And unfortunately, what has happened—I mean for my husband and I personally—we refuse any friends and family from coming to visit us. Because just out of the fear—it has cleaned up a little bit but at one point we never knew when we were going to have to end up on the floor. My mother used to live with us. It was so wild out here that we had to ask her to leave, we had to basically pack her up and ship her out, because we did not want to take that risk.

Victor: Well, this Bullock affair—same thing what you have said happened to her. But she did have some friends over there. They all had to lay on the ground, right out in front of the house there.

Sam: Guy came right out here at the house with a gun in his hand, coming over here toward some kid—I think he was coming over toward Joe I heard later on. And the kids was ducking and dodging and everything you know. Because they thought there was going to be some shooting . . .

Deborah: We live in the Wild, Wild West that we sat on Saturdays and watched.

While this chapter was being drafted, the 11:00 PM news reported the death of a 12-year-old boy on this group's street. The child was apparently shot by a "drive-by" bicyclist. For the participants in this study, there have apparently been sufficient direct experiences of victimization to justify their level of concern.[8]

How do members of these groups interpret crime in terms of its causes and remedies? Which frames best capture and express their understandings of the issue? Chapters 3–6 explore contemporary constructions of crime in the samples of media and popular discourse.

NOTES

1. Specifically, I examined public policy speeches on crime reprinted in *Vital Speeches of the Day* as well as publications of citizen advocacy organizations and think tanks. The latter included the American Enterprise Institute, American Friends Service Committee, Citizens Council on Crime and Delinquency, Citizens for Safety (Boston), Correctional Association of New York, Edna McConnell Clark Foundation, Heritage Foundation, Minnesota Justice Fellowship, National Council on Crime and Delinquency, National Rifle Association and the Public Agenda Foundation.

2. One group of seven, designated as white, included a single African American. Similarly, one group of four, designated as black, included a white Scottish immigrant.

3. Precise figures on the racial compositions of these neighborhoods are not readily available as the tract districts listed in the U.S. Census do not correspond to traditional neighborhood boundaries. But the Census data can be used to generate some basic distinctions: Jamaica Plain has a large Latino population comprising about one-fourth of the total. It also has an African American population that constitutes about another 10%. The South End is the most integrated neighborhood in the sample with almost equal numbers of blacks and whites. Roslindale is the whitest neighborhood with a combined black and Latino population of about 20% (U.S. Census, 1990).

4. The exception is the South End, which consists primarily of brownstone style townhouses and apartment buildings. Two white groups were drawn from this neighborhood.

5. Despite the overrepresentation of women in the study, at least one man participated in each of 17 of the 20 discussions. The three female-only discussions were all in black groups. Appendix C discusses the overrepresentation of women in crime watch groups.

6.   Demographic data for the City of Boston: Sixty three percent of Boston residents are white, 26% African American, and 5% Asian American. Ten percent are of Hispanic descent. Fifty-two percent are female. Thirty percent of Boston residents aged 25 or older hold bachelor's degrees. Fifty-seven percent of adult (20 years and older) Boston residents are aged 20–39, 23% are aged 40–59, and 20% are 60 or older (U.S. Census, 1990). Note that the percentages for the sample population for education and age do not total to 100 because some participants left these items blank on the questionnaire.

7.   Cognitive maps store information about which places are safe and which are not: they therefore "allow people to find their way and provide individuals with a sense of security and safety" (Wachs, 1988:63). The participants' maps seem to have varying degrees of specificity with whites indicating fear of black neighborhoods and blacks indicating fear of specific corners and streets. But participants seem to agree that the segregated minority neighborhoods of Roxbury, Dorchester and Mattapan are the most dangerous in the city. And the actual geographic distribution of homicides is consistent with this widely shared belief (Boston Police Department, 1992).

8.   The postconversation questionnaire asked participants if they had recently been a victim of crime. Thirty-four percent circled "yes" and described a recent crime happening. The crimes mentioned most frequently were house-breaks, purse-snatchings, muggings and car thefts. Several participants mentioned more serious offenses including assaults with knives and shootings.

3

FAULTY SYSTEM

There are many policemen that are doing their job, but it's what happens to these young people when they get to the court and the judges and the lawyers. It's just not right. They're back out on the street. The young man that was shot in Brockton—he was still out on a charge! He was supposed to show up for—What do you call it? Yes, the arraignment. He never did and nobody went looking for him. This criminal justice system needs to be revamped.

—Gloria, an African American woman in her 50s

I think it's an easy solution for conservatives to say "Let's spend more money on law enforcement" and "Let's get tough." [O]ne of the problems with that is it doesn't take into account how much it's going to cost to incarcerate people and how little good incarceration seems to do for people and even for society. So I think we need more social programs . . . But also I think the violent nature of our society contributes. In some ways making our punishment more violent might make things worse and not better.

—Brian, a white man in his mid 20s

The *Faulty System* perspective has its roots in what is commonly known as "classical criminology," most notably in the work of the 18th Century theorist Cesare Beccaria. In his famous essay "On Crimes and Punishments," Beccaria asserts the emerging Enlightenment notion that man is a rational actor whose behavior is governed by the desire to maximize pleasure and minimize pain. This premise concerning human motivation, he insists, leads inexorably to the conclusion that crime stems from irrational laws:

If pleasure and pain are the motives of sensible beings, if, among the motives for even the sublimest acts of men, rewards and punishments were designated by the invisible Legislator, from their inexact distribution arises the contradiction, as little observed as it is common, that the punishments punish crimes which they themselves have occasioned. If an equal punishment be ordained for two crimes that do not equally injure society, men will not be any more deterred from committing the greater crime, if they find a greater advantage associated with it. (1963: 63)

Just as irrational laws encourage crime, so too can rational laws and efficient law enforcement serve to deter it. "Do you want to prevent crime?" Beccaria asks rhetorically, "See to it that the laws are clear and simple and that the entire force of a nation is united in their defense" (Ibid: 94). More specifically, the Italian writer advises, see to it that punishments are certain ("The certainty of a punishment . . . will always make a stronger impression than the fear of another which is more terrible but combined with the hope of impunity"), prompt ("[W]hen the length of time that passes between the punishment and the misdeed is less, so much the stronger and more lasting in the human mind is the association of these two ideas, crime and punishment") and perfectly calibrated to render slightly more pain than the criminal act in question would pleasure (Ibid: 58, 56). In short, where the laws are just and the administration of justice efficient, people will have little cause to engage in crime.

So controversial was "On Crimes and Punishments" in its day that it first appeared under anonymous authorship (Beirne, 1993). The essay, after all, was an implicit challenge to the prevailing Church-sanctioned notion that crime stems from supernatural forces (Pfohl, 1985). Two centuries later, however, many of the ideas expressed in the essay have become so thoroughly naturalized in common sense as to render their polemical content nearly invisible. In this chapter we shall *denaturalize* contemporary expressions of classical criminology, restoring to them some of their argumentative qualities. We turn first to expressions of the perspective in the op ed sample.

FAULTY SYSTEM IN THE OP EDS

An op ed was coded as displaying a positive version of *Faulty System* if it expressed at least one idea element that appears in the coding guide (Appendix B) as either a diagnostic or a prognostic component of the frame. An op ed was coded as displaying a rebuttal of the frame if it expressed an emphatic rejection of at least one of these idea elements.[1] Using these measurement techniques, Figure 3.1 describes *Faulty System's* performance in the op ed sample. The frame was conjured for the purpose of advocacy in 55% of the op eds, and in 36% for the purpose of rebuttal.

These aggregate figures, however, obscure an important distinction between two versions of the frame. One version, which I will call *Lenien-cy*, highlights the putative lax nature of punishment meted out by the criminal justice system; in Beccaria's terms, it attributes crime to insuffi-

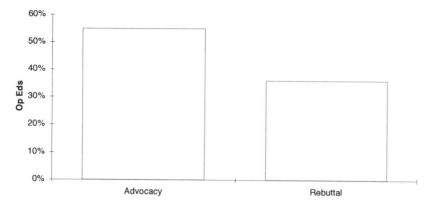

Figure 3.1. Faulty System in the op eds.

cient severity in the treatment of offenders. The other version of the frame, which I will call *Inefficiency*, highlights inconsistencies and inefficiencies in the justice system; in Beccaria's terms, it attributes crime to the system's failure to treat offenders with requisite promptness and certainty.

In the contemporary public discourse, *Leniency* has a decidedly ideological edge; it appears, from a rhetorical standpoint, as the conservative counter-point to the liberal frame *Blocked Opportunities*. *Inefficiency*, on the other hand, appears as purely technical discourse; rhetorically speaking, it is presented as if it were devoid of ideological or political content. In fact, in many cases the frame is implicit in an op ed; the writer merely assumes that crime can be reduced by enhancing the performance of the criminal justice system. In the sections that follow we shall examine the op ed sample for displays of these *subframes* of *Faulty System*.

LENIENCY

As Figure 3.2 indicates, *Leniency* was conjured for the purpose of advocacy in 16% of the op eds and for the purpose of rebuttal in 28%.

Most of the op eds displaying *Leniency* for the purpose of advocacy do so by depicting the punishments currently meted out by the criminal justice system as too lax, or by demanding harsher treatment of offenders. Two rationales for harsher treatment can be discerned in these items. The first is that punishment is necessary to bolster the moral

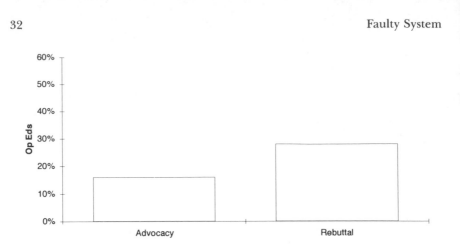

Figure 3.2. Leniency in the op eds.

order. Consider the following example from a *Los Angeles Times* op ed by law professor Samuel Pillsbury:

> When we do not treat offenses such as fraud and burglary and the sale of crack cocaine seriously, we accede to the deterioration of city life. . . . If we care about this violation we should be angry and seek to punish it. Only in this way can we show [the criminal] and ourselves, the extent of our commitment to basic order. (Pillsbury, 1990)*

The second often implicit rationale, is that harsher punishments will *deter* potential offenders. The following example comes from a *Washington Post* op ed by a Judge Reggie Walton, then serving as associate director of the Office of National Drug Control Policy. Walton is criticizing District of Columbia legislation that affords automatic sentence reductions to prison-bound offenders:

> Punishment, or at least the threat of it, has always been used as a deterrent against socially unacceptable behavior. . . . The "Good Time Credit Act" . . . means that . . . the perpetrator of a second degree murder in the District of Columbia will serve only about 10 years in prison for the malicious taking of a human life. . . . I submit that there are many cases where a prison sentence restricted by the law as it is now is the equivalent of a slap on the wrist when compared with the horror of the crime. (Walton, 1990)

Among the op eds displaying positive versions of *Leniency* are also a smaller number that imply the subframe by calling for a relaxation of regulations governing police and prosecutorial conduct. These have in

* Op eds quoted in the text are referenced on pp. 191–2.

common the implicit claim that Fourth and Fifth Amendment protections "handcuff" law enforcement agents, preventing them from performing their order-maintaining functions. The most striking example appeared in the *Los Angeles Times* in the aftermath of the police beating of motorist Rodney King. The writer is Llewellyn H. Rockwell:

> As recently as the 1950s—when street crime was not rampant in America —the police always operated on this principle: No matter the vagaries of the court system, a mugger or rapist knew he faced a trouncing— proportionate to the offense and the offender—in the back of the paddy wagon, and maybe even a repeat performance at the station house. As a result, criminals were terrified of the cops, and our streets were safe. (Rockwell, 1991)

Of the video-taped beating of Rodney King, the same writer observes: "It is not a pleasant sight, of course; neither is cancer surgery."

The rebuttal displays of *Leniency* were more common than the advocacy displays. General rejections of the "law and order" approach to crime control were the most common type. Typically these insisted that "getting tough" is an unpromising strategy either because it fails to address crime's root causes or because it has been tried before and failed. The following from a *Washington Post* op ed by Michael Kinsley is an example of the latter type of argument:

> The U.S. prison population has tripled in the past two decades to more than a million. This country has more of its population behind bars than any other nation with reliable statistics . . .* It is absurd to say the answer to rising crime is locking up even more people for even longer periods, or chopping off more heads. But few politicians can resist. (Kinsley, 1991)

Several additional op eds reject the claim, described above, that Fourth and Fifth Amendment protections "handcuff" the police. They argue, for example, that any erosion of defendants' rights would give police "carte blanche to stop and search any of us . . . for any reason whatever, even though no grounds exist to believe we have done anything wrong" (Leshaw, 1991). Or they challenge the notion that Fourth Amendment protections, such as the exclusionary rule that bars illegally obtained evidence from use in court, in fact reduce the effectiveness of the criminal justice system.

Finally, a few items reject the notion, at the core of *Leniency*, that punishment in the U.S. is in fact lax. Consider the following from a *New*

---

* Russia has since surpassed the U.S. as the nation with the largest share of its population behind bars.

York Times op ed by Donald Lay, Chief Justice of the Eighth Circuit Court
of Appeals.

> [W]e countenance . . . episodes of temporary banishment of individuals to
> horrific and indecent environs in our jails and prisons, and falsely assume
> on their return to society that they will become useful citizens bearing no
> resentment. The criminal justice system is a disgrace to a civilized nation
> that prides itself on decency and the belief in the intrinsic worth of every
> individual. . . . The crimes committed against those who are victimized by
> the system are intolerable. (Lay, 1990)

INEFFICIENCY

As noted, discourse that attributes high rates of crime to failures in
the day-to-day operations of the criminal justice system appears non-
ideological but in fact is the expression of a particular point of view. For
Beccaria, the claim that a well-functioning, rational and efficient criminal justice system can deter crime was contentious, even polemical. That
these ideas are assumed rather than defended in contemporary discourse heightens their potential significance for politics and public policy. We therefore take a close look in this section at how the *Inefficiency*
version of *Faulty System* appears in the op ed sample.

As Figure 3.3 indicates, the subframe *Inefficiency* performed considerably better than *Leniency*. It was conjured for the purpose of advocacy
in 48% of the op eds, and for the purpose of rebuttal in just 12%.

Three categories of advocacy displays can be readily discerned and

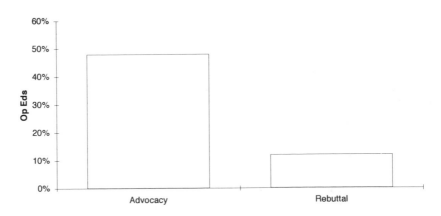

Figure 3.3.   Inefficiency in the op eds.

together account for most instances of this subframe. The first includes items that attribute crime, at least implicitly, to the system's failure to prosecute and sentence offenders swiftly and with certainty. Typical of these is the following excerpt from a *New York Times* op ed by columnist Todd S. Purdum. The author is arguing that the proposed hiring of 5,000 new police officers for New York City cannot, by itself, reduce the city's crime problem.

> In theory, there should be enough prosecutors, probation officers, enough jail guards and jail cells, to handle the problems the police bring in off the streets every day. But virtually no one thinks there are—or that the system they are in works very well. So if more officers are hired and more cells are built, but trial calendars are still clogged, dismissals of serious charges are still common, caseloads for probation workers are still too high, the gap between arrest and arraignment times is still too long and the likelihood of avoiding punishment is still high even for criminals who are caught, what will have changed?

The author's point: "The challenge is to make the whole stubborn sprawling process not just bigger, but better" (Purdum, 1990).

The second category includes items that either complain about the absence of adequate resources for law enforcement or call for more resources. The most common characteristic of these displays is the demand for more cops. The following illustration is from a *Los Angeles Times* piece by columnist Joe Domanick. The author is describing New York City in the aftermath of the stabbing death of Brian Watkins, a tourist from Utah killed while attempting to defend his mother in an attempted subway mugging:

> The outraged talk in the wake of Watkin's killing was rightly of more cops, more judges, more probation officers, more jails, a reemphasis "community policing" and the modernization of the police communications system—all of which New York desperately needs, and all of which can only improve a cynical calcified police force. (Domanick, 1990)

The third category of positive *Inefficiency* displays includes items that call for new approaches to policing and sentencing. Proposed innovations include alternative sentencing, intensive policing of "hot spots," and campaigns to disrupt "open-air" drug markets. But the proposed reform that receives by far the most attention urges that cops be assigned to particular neighborhoods and instructed to walk a daily "beat." Typically described as either "community policing" or "problem oriented policing," this deployment strategy is promoted in 13 (22%) op eds. It is mentioned in the Domanick op ed quoted above, but the following from a *Washington Post* piece by columnist George Will offers a more ample account of the strategy:

> The newfangled notion of "community policing" is essentially the old-fangled notion that more police should get out of their cars and back on the beat. There, they can deal not just reactively with crime, but proactively with the disorders—loitering, poorly parented children, panhandling, anxiety that drives people indoors. These are early indices of neighborhood decay. (Will, 1991)

Inefficiency is rebutted when a writer claims that the performance of the criminal justice system is irrelevant to the volume of crime in society. Rejections of *Inefficiency* are distinct from rejections of *Leniency* in that the latter consist strictly of rejections of harsh and punitive measures ("crack-downs" and "get-tough policies"), whereas the former claim that all law enforcement responses to crime (i.e., even the apparently progressive enforcement strategies such as community policing and alternative sentencing) are unpromising. The following illustration is from a *Washington Post* op ed. The writer is James J. Fyfe, a former New York City police lieutenant and current American University professor:

> The experience of Washington demonstrates the futility of over reliance on law enforcement as a crime control strategy. In about 18 months, D.C. police made 46,000 arrests—one for every 14 District residents—in Operation Cleansweep, the recent anti-drug operation. . . . [D]rugs are still readily available, the violence associated with the drug traffic shows no sign of abating and the major result apparently was to clog the courts and correctional system. (Fyfe, 1991)

Effective crime control, in Fyfe's view, can only be accomplished through fundamental changes in society. Criminal justice institutions, no matter how massive, cannot make the society significantly more safe.

Next we turn to the frame's performance in the peer group discussions.

FAULTY SYSTEM IN THE DISCUSSIONS

Our measurement strategy for assessing frame performance in the discussions is quite simple: Where discussion participants expressed unanimous support for a frame, we will regard its performance as "strong." Where participants disagreed with one another over a frame's merits (that is, where at least one group member staked out a cogent position contrary to the others with respect to the frame), we will regard its performance as "mixed." Finally, where participants were unanimous

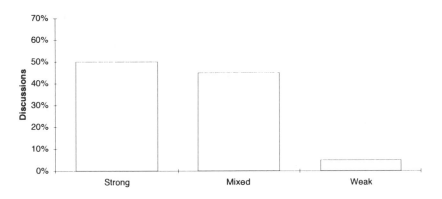

Figure 3.4. Faulty System in the discussions.

in their rejection of a frame, we will regard its performance as "weak." Using these measurement criteria, Figure 3.4 describes *Faulty System's* performance in the discussions.

The chart indicates that participants in 50% of the discussions expressed unanimous support for *Faulty System* whereas in 5% they unanimously rejected the frame. In the remaining 45% of the discussions participants disagreed with one another over the frame's merits.

As Figure 3.5 indicates, racial differences were quite modest: 57% of the black and 37% of the white groups unanimously embraced the frame. Given the size of the sample, these differences cannot be regarded as significant.

The distinction between *Leniency* and *Inefficiency* proved unhelpful in illuminating the dynamics of *Faulty System's* performance in the conversational discourse. While the distinction taps into a natural fault line in

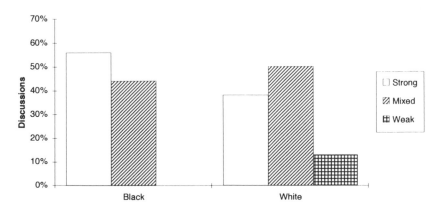

Figure 3.5. Faulty Systems in the discussions, by race.

the op ed discourse, it finds no such fault line in the peer group discussions. Discussion participants, it turns out, tended to conflate the subframes, often expressing elements of both in individual utterances. This state of affairs militated against any attempt to quantify the subframes' relative prominence in the discussions. What should become clear in the following account, however, is that rhetoric associated with *Leniency* was considerably more prominent in the peer group discussions than in the op ed sample.

SUPPORTIVE ARGUMENTS

How did discussion participants conjure *Faulty System?* How does their discourse compare with the discourse of the op ed writers? We will consider six lines of argument, each one advanced by participants in at least two discussions.

Revolving Door Justice

The most common line of argument attributes urban crime to the putatively poor performance of the court system. Attributions of this sort were expressed in *all* of the black, seven of the white and two of the mixed groups. In only two groups, both comprised largely of highly credentialed professionals, was harsh criticism of the courts altogether absent.

Discourse on the shortcomings of the courts advanced the claims that offenders "fall through the cracks" or escape punishment altogether (13 discussions); that the punishments meted out are too lax and time actually served too short (13 discussions); that judges are too liberal and "out of touch" (6 discussions); that the judicial process is too slow (5 discussions); and that sentences are random but ought to be uniform (3 discussions). Because these claims are so important to the participants' constructions of the problem of crime, we should consider several examples. The first comes from the discussion of a white, mostly working-class group. It includes instances of the first three claims described above.

Group: Gordon Road
Cast:

Sally, retired, in her late 60s or early 70s.
Rhoda, a secretary and high school graduate, in her late 50s.
Edward, a corporate environmental manager and college graduate, in his mid 40s.

Christine, an administrative assistant and high school graduate, in her early 20s.
Martha, retired, in her late 60s or early 70s.

Facilitator:	O.K. Next question. "Do you think the crime problem is getting worse or better and why?"
Edward:	I think it's getting worse to some extent, because the hands of the police and the judicial system— not so much the judicial system—the hands of the police and the prison system are somewhat tied, so that the punishment is almost a joke.
Sally:	Doesn't fit the crime.
Edward:	And if you're a hardcore criminal, you don't really get punished.
Rhoda:	When a police officer makes an arrest, before he finishes his paperwork, the damn criminal is back on the street.
Unknown Voice:	Right. I know.
Rhoda:	The courts have no room for them. There's no follow-up.
Christine:	It's easy to be a criminal.
Rhoda:	Jails. The courts don't follow through. They're let out on the street, and then the cop doesn't even finish his paperwork and the guy's back out on the street. Ninety percent of the cops don't even want to go to court anymore. It's not worth the effort.
Edward:	It's discouraging.
Rhoda:	It is. They're discouraged. I mean when we were assaulted, Christine and I, the cop literally said, do you want to push this? Yeah, I want him off the street! Of course I want to push it!
Edward:	And the judicial system is very set up to protect the rights—But you're far more protected if you're a criminal than if you're a victim, which is very frustrating.
Unknown Voice:	Mmhm.
Martha:	You're telling the truth.

[A few pages further down in the transcript:]

Martha:	The police make the arrests, but nothing happens. If you're a policeman and you arrested a hardened criminal, and you're sitting in court

and all of a sudden this sweetheart of a judge says—
"There's a little bit of good in everybody." If he knew
how little there was in some of them, he wouldn't sleep
nights! So the little so-and-so gets–goes free. And he
goes out and he does it again. He says, what do I have
to worry about? I can commit this crime many times.
And they do. They do. They keep repeating their
crime, because they have no fear.

The next example of discourse critical of the courts comes from a
black group. In this excerpt, Margaret charges that punishments meted
out by the courts are both too lax and insufficiently uniform. The participants are responding to the statement used to trigger the frame (see
Appendix A, question 3, statement 1):

Group: Peach Tree Lane
Cast:

Margaret, retired, African American, in her early 60s.
William, an organizer, Latino, in his 30s.

Margaret:	I think that the court system needs to be reformed. I think that we need a different kind of parole system. We need to make parole less available. I mean if you're gonna get ten years, you should get almost ten years.
William:	Not two and a half.
Margaret:	Not take off what you've served already in detention, then parole you because—
William:	You've been a good boy!
Margaret:	—for a year or so. And you're out in two. Or two and a half. You know what I mean? And you were supposed to serve ten. I think that if the crime was big enough for ten, you should be serving almost ten. So I think we need a—I think we really need to reform the parole system. Then as we were just saying, we need to reform the educational system in the prisons. And also I think that judges should more or less have the same kind of sentencing procedure, not one judge say two years and somebody else does the same crime, ten years! You know what I mean?
William:	More uniform.

Margaret: More uniform procedure, and set limits. They can't go
              under this limit, like if that crime should be five years
              then it would be five years. Some judge say three in-
              stead, because of some circumstances he finds. No, it's
              five years. Five years in all courts. Maybe he wants to go
              to six or seven, but he can't go to four.

The final example of discourse critical of the courts comes from the
discussion of a white group. In this excerpt the conversationalists charge
that offenders often escape punishment altogether, and that terms of
imprisonment, when actually administered, are too short. They are also
responding to the trigger statement.

Group: Jacob's Lane
Cast: (See p. 1)
New Addition:

Peg, a college instructor with more than a college degree, in her late 20s.

   Peg: I agree somewhat. Because I was in the crime watch in J.P.
              [a Boston neighborhood], where a guy had done over 30
              house break-ins. They caught him over 30 times for break-
              ing into houses. And it was finally when a group of people
              who in the neighborhood got together to go against that
              guy in court, they went down there, they stood up and they
              said to the judge, if this kid is let go with a slap on the hand
              one more time, he's going to be lynched by us. And that kid
              got sent to jail. So I think that's partly the answer. On the
              other hand, I also don't think that jails are reforming
              people.
Carol: It's a complicated question, because, I think, I agree with
              Peg that, you know, it would be wonderful if our criminal
              justice system worked, and it did the things it was supposed
              to do. But we know very well that it's a revolving door and
              you get them in jail, and what the hell good does it do? You
              know, makes them harder criminals.
  Alex: And plus they're out in no time. I mean—
Carol: You do everything but shoot down the entire city of Cleve-
              land, and you'll be out in 6 to 8, you know?
  Alex: Exactly. If not less. You go in the front door, and two hours
              later your lawyer's in with the bail until trial or whatever,
              and you're out.

Finally, note that criticism of the courts was frequently expressed through slogans. For example, participants in numerous discussions exclaimed that punishment amounts to a "slap on the wrist;" that the courts and prisons have "revolving doors" or "turnstyles;" that "if you do the crime, you should do the time;" that "the justice system protects the rights of criminals but not the rights of victims;" and that because of court procedures, crime victims are "victimized twice."

Adult Crimes, Kiddy Punishments

Participants in more than half of the groups also conjured the frame by arguing that young people commit crimes because they know that as juveniles they will be treated with Leniency. Claims concerning the consequences of the system's alleged Leniency with youthful offenders were made in six black (66%), three white (37%), and two mixed groups. While the sample size is too small to permit a definitive judgment on the significance of these racial differences, the rhetoric on the treatment of youthful offenders seems more important to the discourse of the African American group members. We take our first example from one of their discussions. In the following excerpt, the participants are responding to question 2 (see Appendix A):

Group: Fisher Hill
Cast: (See p. 25)

Deborah: The antiquated judicial system . . . is not in line with what is going on today. The laws around juveniles. They commit adult crimes and yet they get kiddy punishment. And I think for the most part juveniles are the big problem.

Chuck: They lean on this. They lean on this. You find these kids know the law better than the defense attorneys.

[clamor and laughter]

Karl: When they turn them out, tell them to turn them out in a suburb. They won't do that. They turn them out and turn them right back on us. And they come back and take revenge out on us!

[A few pages further down in the transcript:]

Yeah, it's falling right back to the same thing. We have to make them accountable, that's all.

Georgia: And they have to be responsible for their own actions, especially when they get to a certain age. What is the age of reason, all right? Come off it. You've had kids out here, 15, 16, 17-years-old with guns. And they're going to sit here, and they're going to shoot somebody and say, oh, I'm sorry, I didn't mean to hit that person? No, no. It doesn't work. You know what a gun is used for, you treat [it as an] adult crime.

Our second example of discourse on the system's alleged permissiveness toward youthful offenders comes from the discussion of the group at Jacob's Lane. It appears just one page down in the transcript from the excerpt quoted above.

Laura: I think there is some truth [to that]. I think young kids, the 13, 14, 15-year-olds, I think they feel "We can do whatever we want and get away with it." I think if they have a fear of being taken off the street or taken away from home and sent somewhere—I don't mean like a jail or—

Alex: No.

Laura: —but somewhere, it would deter them. I think the feeling [is] that they can do anything and get away with it.

Alex: There was a girl on the news. She was 15-years-old and she was caught for robbery, and the newsman was interviewing her and she said—That's exactly what she said—She said "I can do anything I want till I'm 18 because I'll just get right back on the street because I'm underage." And I thought, what an attitude! That's what it is, they think they can get away with it.

How should the criminal justice system handle youthful offenders? In the view of many participants, after the "age of reason," juvenile offenders should be sentenced as if they were adults.

Luxury Prisons

Participants also conjured the frame by depicting prisons as excessively pleasant. Reading the transcripts, one learns that prisons offer "three hots and a cot," a chance to "pump up," air conditioning, swimming pools, parking garages with mosaic floors, opportunities for higher education, special rooms for sexual liaisons, top quality medical care and a host of other amenities unavailable to most Americans. Always implicit in this type of discourse—and often explicit—is the notion that harsher prisons could more effectively deter crime.

Claims concerning the high quality of prison life were advanced in four white, four black and all three mixed groups. They were almost always expressed in an animated fashion and often sparked laughter. The example that follows is by no means extraordinary in its tenor or ideational content. It comes from the discussion of the Fisher Hill group quoted in the previous section. The cast is the same but for the addition of Lloyd, a Cape Verdean police officer who works for the Registry of Motor Vehicles. He is a high school graduate and is in his mid 30s.

Deborah:	There's no rehabilitation services available, or no deterrent services either. Because we were talking earlier about quadruple bunking them for example. You know, make prison a really—
Lloyd:	Not a kiddy club.
Deborah:	Yeah. A real terrible place to be—
Karl:	Take away the TV.
Lloyd:	The gyms, the swimming pools—
Georgia:	Let them know that they're there for a reason.
Lloyd:	[Take away] the cable TV's.
Deborah:	[Over clamor] If they're going to act like animals, they should be treated like animals.
Lloyd:	People here in the Winter have it so bad that they'd rather go into jail because it's so good there. Three squares. A place to work out. A place to watch TV. A place to go swimming, or whatever. And read and get a little bit of knowledge and stuff, and then it's warm. And then they come out in the summertime.
Georgia:	And if they're there long enough, they can come out with a Ph.D.
Unknown voice:	Mmhm.

[A few paragraphs later, in response to the trigger statement:]

Lloyd:	I feel strongly on that one. That one is something that has to be addressed. That's why we're trying to make more prisons and stuff like that. But they need to make them less plush, right? And more of them.
Unknown voice:	Mmhm.
Chuck:	Make it what it is—it's a jail. [Over clamor] It's a prison.
Unknown Voice:	Quadruple bunk 'em.
Chuck:	It's not a country club. It's not a camp. It's not a summer camp, you know. It's not body building

	camp. You know, most of these guys go in the joint, they come out, they look like Arnold Schwarzenegger.
Unknown Voice:	Sure you're right. Sure you're right.
Unknown Voice:	Pumping iron every day.
Unknown Voice:	Eating good.
Chuck:	If you don't want to work, you don't have to work.
Karl:	You know how much it costs a year to keep one in prison?
Deborah:	Something outrageous.
Karl:	$46,000.
Deborah:	More than they pay me.
Lloyd:	Is it?
Karl:	To keep *one*. $46,000 for *one*.
Deborah:	Wow.

In only one discussion was the notion that prisons are too cushy directly challenged by a group member. For the most part, the observation was treated as a common place.

Handcuffed Police

Faulty System was keyed in one third of the groups through the claim that police officers, prosecutors and prison officials are prevented from performing their jobs by senseless definitions of offenders' "rights." Instances of this basic argument allege that offenders are set free because of "technicalities," that the "hands of the police are tied," and that the public must choose between "civil rights and public safety." One example appears above, in the lengthy excerpt from the discussion of the Gordon Road group. Later in that same discussion, a participant makes the point about "rights" even more explicitly:

Rhoda:	[T]hey took away a lot from the police when all these civil rights came in. When I [was] a kid growing up and a cop came down the street, the beat cop came down the street, there wasn't a kid on the block that didn't shake in his shoes, so that there wouldn't be anything wrong.

In all, claims that a putative preoccupation with offenders' rights is a source of crime could be heard in three black, two white and two mixed groups. The most cogent and elaborate form of the argument was expressed by Henry, an African American police officer. In the following excerpt he is responding to the statement used to trigger the frame:

Group: Grove Hills Parkway

Henry: The communities further neutralize the police by emphasizing the importance of not violating people's rights.
We're in the middle of a war zone and people are acting
like animals feeding off of the life of other people. Yet you
want to worry about that person's rights? So the police in
response have to. Now you have a police department that's
ineffective. That's another feather in the animal's hat. He
can really do what he wants more now. It's not the police's
fault. . . . The courts can't prosecute. And certain judges
will go along with the emphasis on rights and rights and
rights. So these people have the right to rip you off. The
right to stay out there. The right not to be dealt with by the
system. . . . [Later in the discussion:] [O]ur Boston police
department has been watered down. It is really not that
effective. And it doesn't have the backing of the community at all. They have to make up their minds what the hell
they want. Do they want law and order or do they want
civil rights for the guys that are running around that rip
you and your family off?

Officer Friendly

Participants in more than half of the groups conjured the frame by
recommending that police be assigned to particular neighborhoods and
instructed to walk a daily "beat." They argued that effective policing
requires visibility, commitment and a good relationship with neighborhood residents. These interests, they insisted, are undermined by the
practice of patrolling by police cruiser. Officers who walk a daily beat can
get to know their assigned turf, learn who the troublemakers are, and
inspire confidence in neighborhood residents.

The participants' discourse on this topic was strikingly similar to the
public discourse on "community policing." In fact, in many groups participants used the term "community policing," indicating a familiarity
with the public discourse. Consider the following illustration excerpted
from the discussion of a white group.

Group: Hallibut Square
Cast:

Bob, a housekeeping supervisor and high school graduate, in his early 40s.
Phyllis, a high school graduate in her late 40s.
Janet, a medical billing clerk and high school graduate, in her late 40s.

Bob: Well, like there's no cops around no more.
Phyllis: This is true.
Bob: Like when we did have the horse guy, he went off at 11:00 or whatever it was.
Phyllis: Yeah, he probably went on vacation and the horse went on vacation too.

[Later in the discussion:]

Janet: But I think too that more people on the Hill should work with the police than just the few of us that do . . . I mean like this new community policing thing. Because people don't get to know the police and the police are supposed to drop off at people's houses to come in and say, Hi, how are you? What's been going on in the area?—stop by for five minutes, ten minutes—whatever. But because people don't get involved, they're not going to know about it so there's not going to be any residences that the police can stop at and we have to have that. We have to have the policeman know the area. And besides we need to know the police. Cause then they get used to you. And they're gonna fight more, to make sure that this is their territory, and that their territory is protected.

Racial differences do not appear significant with respect to discourse on community policing: Calls for a renewed emphasis on foot patrols, and so on, could be heard in four black, six white and one mixed group.

Discourse on community policing often featured nostalgic references to an "officer friendly," a beat cop fondly remembered from a participant's past. The images conveyed in these references are more typical of discourse displaying the frame *Social Breakdown*. This is hardly surprising as the "beat cop" is remembered as much for his role as an informal agent of social control as for his formal duties an agent of the state. Consider the following illustration; the speaker is Stella, a white homemaker in her 70s.

Group: Maple Street

Stella: Well, I think it would be helpful if the policemen that we do have could relate to the neighborhoods a little better than they do. We have cruisers coming down here. They come down and turn around—whip up the street again all the time. And I do think the walking cop I grew up with— Casey, the cop living right behind, down the next street— when my brother Alex was in trouble, which was not very great trouble but you know, running into a neighbor's yard,

taking pears off a tree and stuff like that—Casey delighted
in coming to the Protestant minister's home—yes he did!—
and we were good friends, but nothing pleased him more
than to come and report to my father than Alex was in
trouble again. And he was in a lot of trouble that way. But I
do think maybe if the police were walking and getting acquainted with the neighborhood—And then, speaking of
our neighborhood here . . . [Stella shifts to a new topic.]

In addition to the relatively mild criticisms of police officers' reliance
on radio cruisers, participants in eight groups expressed much more
serious criticisms of police performance. Charges that the police target
minority men for harassment are associated with the frame *Racist System*
and discussed in Chapter 6. Here we are concerned with claims that the
police are corrupt, ineffective, or deployed disproportionately in neighborhoods with relatively little crime. Race differences with respect to
these kinds of criticisms are striking: As Figure 3.6 indicates, discourse
charging ineffectiveness, corruption, and unfair deployment could be
heard in six black groups (66%) but in just one white group (12.5%). In
addition, such criticisms were expressed in one mixed group, by an
African American participant.

What makes these race differences still more striking is that in three
white but only one black group participants spontaneously rejected the
notion that the police bear any responsibility for the crime problem
(Gloria's contribution to the epigram for this chapter is the only example
of an African American exonerating the police). Let us first consider two
brief illustrations of discourse critical of police performance. Both are
excerpted from the discussion of a black group. The first speaker is an
African American school teacher in her mid 30s:

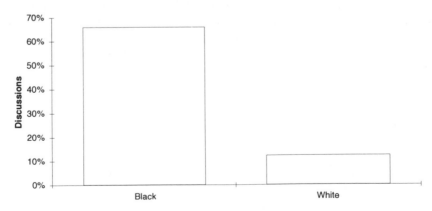

Figure 3.6.   Groups charging police ineffectiveness, corruption.

Group: Pleasant Street

Sharlene: [P]eople don't trust anyone today, and that means a policeman, because some of the policemen are committing the same crime as all the people that they arrest! [Right!—a voice interjects] And some of the judges are committing the same crimes. We need an enema— as what's his name would say. [laughter] It's just so many things that need to happen. And I don't see it happening—in my lifetime.

The second speaker is an Hispanic office manager in her early 30s.

Priscilla: The patrol cars sitting around Dunkin' Donuts, two and three at a time. Maybe they should [stop] doing that and go on patrol and do what they're supposed to do. And stop bothering people because they're giving them a parking ticket. Just silly things, you know. Get into the real things that they should be—I mean, I got robbed. I had to wait almost an hour to get a policeman over here. He was probably doing something else that was unnecessary, you know. They should restructure and put into priorities what should be done.

Next we consider a brief example of a spontaneous *rejection* of the notion that police bear responsibility for the crime problem. The excerpt is from the discussion of a white group. Note that in addition to illustrating a rejection of police responsibility, the excerpt also presents discourse critical of the putative permissiveness of judges. The speakers are responding to the statement used to trigger the frame.

Group: Dean Avenue
Cast:

Susan, a clerk and high school graduate, in her early 40s.
Bill, a disabled worker who did not finish high school, in his late 40s.

Bill: I've listened to police officers and they've told me that they'll get the criminal and get him to court and the judge gives him a slap on the wrist . . .

Susan: Because the judge gets his bed count in the morning.

Unknown voice: Where are they gonna put 'em if they don't have the room?

> *Susan:* [Apparently mimicking a judge:] "We locked up
> 21 people today because we only had 21 vacant
> beds."
> *Bill:* I don't think it's the police officer, that they're not
> doing their job.
> *Susan:* No. They're bringing them in.
> *Bill:* It's that the judges aren't doing their job.
> *Susan:* But there again it goes around to every time they
> want to build a prison, who wants the prison in
> their backyard? Me, for one, I would love one in
> my backyard. You know why? Because when they
> break out, do you think they're going to stay in
> your backyard? No, they're going to the next
> town.
>
> [laughter]

Bill and Susan agree: The police are bringing in the offenders. It is judges, and perhaps those who oppose new prison construction, that are responsible for the crime problem.

Just Pay the Edison Bill*

Calls for the death penalty, expressed in one black and three white groups, comprised the sixth line of argument by which the frame was expressed in multiple discussions. In the white groups, the death penalty was proposed as a way to relieve prison overcrowding and save on the costs of long-term incarceration. In two discussions, the exchanges on the topic were at once extremist in their ideational content and suffused with humor. The illustration that follows comes from the discussion of the group at Hallibut Square, first introduced earlier in this chapter:

> *Bob:* They should just bring back capital punishment.
> That would give us more room in the jails.
> *Unknown voice:* That would be great.
> *Phyllis:* Well, they have to give some funding to the
> courts, too, because everybody is just passing the
> buck. First of all, you don't have any probation
> officers.

* Boston Edison is the local power utility.

> *Bob:* All you have to do is pay the Edison bill for the electric chair.
>
> *Janet:* No, we'll do it by injection. It will be cheaper.
>
> [laughter]

* * * * *

Three final observations deserve brief mention. First, in two black and one white group participants spontaneously called for the creation of more "boot camp" style detention centers for juvenile or first-time offenders. Second, in one white and two mixed groups participants spontaneously called for harsher punishment for white collar offenders. Third, in three black (but no white or mixed) groups participants expressed support for a curfew for minors.

Next we turn to the rebuttal displays of the frame.

REBUTTAL ARGUMENTS

Faulty System was unanimously rejected by the members of one group and at least one of its core claims was contested in nine others. But in the latter nine groups, typically only one or two voices were raised against the frame. Nevertheless, it is possible to discern several lines of argument against the frame that appeared in numerous discussions. The most important of these insists that the criminal justice system is essentially irrelevant to the question of crime. According to participants in seven groups, crime is caused by social factors and must be treated in terms of its causes. Even if all offenders were imprisoned, crime would persist because its social causes would remain unchanged. Consider the following example from the discussion of a mixed group. The speaker is an African American woman in her 30s or 40s.[2]

Group: Troy Street

> *Vanessa:* I agree with you Michael. Certainly we need to deal with the people that do commit crimes—need to suffer the consequences. By focusing your money and your energy and your people on putting these people in jail, *it's like closing the door after the horse is gone.* You know? You just need to refocus. You need to focus your efforts elsewhere, you need to focus on prevention. You need to focus on helping kids refocus their energies. Helping families stay together. Helping families get jobs. Hous-

ing. Education. It's like closing the barn door after the
horse is gone.

The second most important rebuttal argument rejects the frame because of its implicit sanction of police abuses, especially those perpe-
trated upon African American men. (This argument, in addition to
rebutting *Faulty System*, conjures the frame *Racist System;* the relevant
passages were therefore cross-coded under both frames). It was expressed in four black but in none of the white or mixed groups. Our
example is drawn from a speech by Alice, an African American high
school graduate, in her 30s. She is responding to the trigger statement:

Group: Longwood Road

Alice: I mean, there's holes in all that. If you agreed, that means
that all the black men in Boston are gonna be picked up,
stripped, searched, and thrown in jail and doing time for a
lot of things they haven't committed.

Arguments against capital punishment were treated as negations of
the frame and constitute the third argument against it. Such arguments
were expressed in one black, two white and one mixed group. In contrast
to the discourse advocating the expansion of capital punishment, these
rebuttal arguments were generally offered in brief utterances and in
tones that were affectively neutral. They pointed out, for example, that
evidence of a deterrent effect for capital punishment is scant; that if an
innocent is executed the error cannot be corrected; and that executions
intensify the "climate of violence" and thereby generate more crime.

The final rebuttal argument, appearing in just two white groups,
insists that the "get tough" approach to crime has proved costly and
ineffective. Not only does incarceration fail to bring down the crime
rate; in fact, by hardening offenders, it makes matters worse. An example of this type of argument appears as Brian's contribution to the
epigram for this chapter.

CONCLUSION

The evidence presented in this chapter lends a good deal of support
to the conventional wisdom about public opinion on crime. For starters,
the frame that holds the criminal justice system responsible for crime
was expressed in more than half of the op eds; more frequently, as we
shall see, than any of its rival frames. What's more, *Faulty System* also
performed well in the discussions: Its claims were expressed without

dissent in half of the groups, and in the 40% in which they were contested, the voices raised in opposition were affectless, curt, and typically in the minority.

Beyond these general findings, however, were some interesting details. To fully grasp *Faulty System's* dynamic performance in the public discourse I found it necessary to distinguish between two subframes. The subframe *Inefficiency* performed quite strongly; it was displayed for the purpose of advocacy in 48% of the op eds, four times as frequently as for the purpose of rebuttal. The subframe *Leniency*, however, did not perform nearly so well. It was displayed nearly twice as frequently for the purpose of rebuttal as for the purpose of advocacy.

Although the nature of the popular discourse discouraged any attempt to quantify the relative prominence of the subframes, as the account offered above should have made clear, both perspectives proved quite resonant. Calls for the death penalty and harsher punishments for juvenile offenders, and complaints about liberal judges, defendants' rights and the allegedly cushy quality of prison life, all indicate a strong showing for *Leniency*. At the same time, complaints about clogged courts, overcrowded prisons and inadequate police protection likewise indicate a strong performance for *Inefficiency*.

Comparing the public and popular discourse, we see that the most noteworthy difference concerns *Leniency*. While the subframe's ideational content was more often rejected than affirmed in the op ed sample, the opposite proved true with respect to the peer group discussions.

Finally, though not discussed in this chapter, the reader may have noticed that the conversational discourse expressing *Faulty System* draws heavily upon news stories, mass mediated "facts" (by which I mean fact claims) and the personal experiences of the participants. The significance of this state of affairs will be examined in Chapters 7 and 8. In the following chapter, we turn to discourse on the frame *Social Breakdown*.

NOTES

1. Op eds that expressed elements of multiple frames were treated as displaying multiple frames. For example, an op ed that attributed crime to bad parenting and called for the implementation of a new policing strategy would have been coded as displaying both *Social Breakdown* and *Faulty System*.

2. Vanessa departed the discussion session without completing the postdiscussion questionnaire; further biographical information is therefore unavailable.

SOCIAL BREAKDOWN

*Basically the reason [we have so much crime] is because society's whole moral struc-
ture and moral fiber has broken down, where people don't feel like they have to live by
the rules or that they have to nurture their neighbor or, you know, whatever.*

—Jenny, a white woman in her 30s

*[T]he sad and unfortunate part to me is when I hear concerns talking about how you
have to keep the family together. . . . It's almost like their emphasis is on this ideal
that doesn't exist. You know—Ozzie and Harriet don't exist anymore in America. . . . And they're always talking about the black community, how the family's
disintegrating. And if I've heard that term once, I've heard it a zillion times!*

—Vanessa, an African American woman in her 30s

The *Social Breakdown* perspective has its social scientific roots in the
work of the early "Chicago School" researchers Robert Park, Ernest
Burgess, Clifford Shaw and Henry McKay. In a number of studies extending from the 1920s to the 1950s, the Chicago sociologists examined
the impact of rapid social change on various urban neighborhoods. Advancing what became known in the literature of criminology as "social
disorganization theory," they argued that rapid change destroys the prevailing normative order and thereby produces crime and delinquency.
Under pressure from immigration, industrialization and urbanization,
families and communities lose their ability to regulate individual conduct. Moral dissensus results, which in turn opens the door to crime and
delinquency. The problem is especially acute with respect to children
growing up in the communities closest to the center of the city. "Children
living in such communities" Shaw and McKay explain, "are exposed to a
variety of contradictory standards and forms of behavior rather than to
a relatively consistent and conventional pattern" (Pfohl, 1985:150).

For many of the early social disorganization theorists, the solution to
the social problems that resulted from rapid social change could be
found in purposive efforts by ordinary people to *reorganize* their communities. Several Chicago School figures were, in fact, instrumental in
organizing the Chicago Area Project, an agency that prefigured the

community action projects of the 1960s and 1970s, innovating many of the tactics commonly associated with urban organizing today. The Project sponsored counseling and recreational activities aimed at adolescents and coordinated the community improvement activities of schools, churches, social clubs, labor unions and local businesses. Linking these efforts was the basic theoretical notion that the best way to combat the erosion of informal social control is to organize community members to reassert their leadership and in so doing to establish a new and binding moral order (Ibid).

Contemporary discourse that attributes crime to community and family breakdown conjures the arguments of the theorists of social disorganization. While new contests have emerged over the contemporary roots of disorganization, the imagery of the Chicago theorists remains as potent today as ever. We turn first to traces of this imagery in the contemporary public discourse.

SOCIAL BREAKDOWN IN THE OP EDS

Figure 4.1 compares the performances of *Faulty System* and *Social Breakdown* in the op ed sample. As we can see, *Social Breakdown* was substantially less visible than *Faulty System;* it appeared in a positive light in 36% of the columns as compared to 55% for *Faulty System.* But *Social Breakdown* was also less likely to be rejected by the columnists; it was conjured for the purpose of rebuttal in 5% of the columns in comparison with 36% for *Faulty System.*

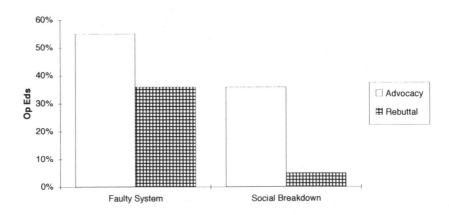

Figure 4.1.   Faulty System and Social Breakdown in the op eds.

We can discern four types of advocacy displays of *Social Breakdown*. The first two advance the frame's diagnostic component; one attributes crime to family breakdown, the other to community disintegration. The third and fourth types advance the frame's prognostic component; one calls for various kinds of interventions (rehabilitation, counseling, "boot camps") aimed at setting offenders on the straight and narrow; the other for collective action by neighborhood residents to reduce crime.

Several op eds presented the frame through a combination of two or three of these arguments thereby attesting to the gestalt-like coherence of the larger perspective. A particularly pure example of this tendency appeared in a *Washington Post* op ed by Chief Justice Richard Neely of the West Virginia Court of Appeals. Consider the following excerpt:

> Crime, I believe, emerges from a breakdown of the traditional family and traditional neighborhood. If that sounds tiredly familiar, let me add this: Currently, 72 percent of all women with minor children at home work full time. Who's watching the neighborhood after school? The very act of organizing to protect a neighborhood from crime has the effect of strengthening traditional values concerning standards of public behavior. (Neely, 1990)

For Neely, as for the social disorganization theorists, crime results from an erosion in the informal controls normally imposed by family and community. The solution, Neely believes, lies in collective action to re-establish adult moral authority.

Surprisingly perhaps, attributions for crime to family breakdown or negligent parenting were relatively rare, appearing—including the Neely piece—in just three op eds (5%). Attributions to community breakdown, appearing in seven op eds (17%), were actually much more common. Interestingly, in many of the latter, columnists told the story of Kitty Genovese, the New York City woman who in 1964 was stabbed to death while dozens of her neighbors watched passively from their windows. Genovese apparently serves as a condensing symbol for the problems of community breakdown and urban anonymity. Consider this example from a *Washington Post* op ed by Richard Cohen:

> The saga of Kitty Genovese became a national story. The dead woman came to personify the cold anonymity of the big city, its lack of community, its indifference. . . . We have learned, often the hard way, that New York is not atypical. (Cohen, 1991)

Columnists also evoked the frame by expressing its prognostic component. In four op eds (7%) they called for rehabilitation and counseling programs, recreation centers and "boot camps"—all interventions that

share in common the tacit claim that crime stems from inadequate supervision or a failure of moral integration. In nine op eds (16%) they promoted the notion that ordinary people ought to band together, in
cooperation with the police, to fight crime. Most of the items featuring
this latter line of argument urged a greater "police-community partnership" against crime.[1] The following example is from a *Boston Globe* column by City Councilor Charles Yancey:

> We all share some of the responsibility to create a safer environment. The
> problems cannot be solved by the police alone. The police risk their lives
> every day for those who live in Boston. Community residents who demon-
> strate great courage in the face of rising violence, also cannot solve the
> problem alone. We need to develop a partnership between city govern-
> ment and community residents. This partnership must be based on mutual
> respect and support. . . . The public must be involved in the fight against
> violence. There are hundreds of community crime watch groups through-
> out the city—especially in Dorchester, Mattapan, and Roxbury—eager to
> work with the police. (Yancey, 1991)

In addition, in several others, columnists simply called for ordinary
people to "get involved" in crime-fighting activities. For example, consider the following from a *New York Times* op ed. The writer is Todd
Watkins, the brother of the tourist from Utah whose killing sparked
widespread media attention.

> [W]e challenge you, the citizens of New York, to get involved. . . . If every-
> one would take the time to get involved, to report crimes when you see
> them, criminals would be apprehended and the crime rate would go down.
> (Watkins, 1990)

Finally, columnists can inflect *Social Breakdown* with either a liberal or
a conservative accent. When they attribute social breakdown to poverty,
capital flight or deindustrialization—in other words, when in a single
argument they conflate *Social Breakdown* with *Blocked Opportunities*—they
are inflecting the frame in a liberal fashion. This sort of display appeared in three items in the op ed sample. The following from the Fyfe
op ed first quoted in Chapter 3 is an example:

> The increase [in crime] can be attributed to several converging forces, but
> two probably are most important. The huge baby-boom generation en-
> tered adolescence, so that an unusually large percentage of the population
> was in its most crime-prone years. In addition, cities changed. For years,
> blacks and Hispanics had steadily been replacing white city dwellers who
> had fled to the suburbs, taking businesses and jobs with them. This pattern
> came to a head in the 1960s, when communities broke up, to be replaced

by densely populated projects. Urban tax bases eroded, municipal services declined and all the ills of the inner city flourished as they had not since the great waves of European immigration a half-century earlier. (Fyfe, 1991)

The frame can also be inflected with a conservative accent. This can be achieved by attributing breakdown to welfare dependency, permissive parenting, or the putative cultural and social effects of the protest movements of the 1960s and 1970s. Indeed, these are precisely the kinds of attributions preferred by many conservative intellectuals and their think tanks.[2] But the op ed sample does not include any frame displays of this type.

There were just three rebuttal displays of the frame. One insisted that rehabilitation ("Lock of the criminals, teach them the good life, mold them into law abiding citizens and then let them go") has "failed miserably" (Mokhiber, 1990). The other two criticized the notion that ordinary people ought to engage in crime-fighting. An instance of this latter argument appeared in the *New York Times* as a contribution by playwright Janusz Glowacki. It was written in response to Mayor Dinkins' call, appearing in an op ed two weeks earlier, for the "calm assistance of every citizen of New York" in the war against crime. Glowacki's piece is entitled "Sorry, I'm No Crime Fighter."

The enthusiasm of good people, I suspect, is rarely efficient when confronted with guns and skillful criminals. I would like to point out, for example, that President Bush didn't ask the Saudis to arm themselves with baseball bats and walkie talkies and stand on their border. The President applied a more traditional strategy: he mobilized the Army, Navy, Air Force and Marines. I'm ashamed to admit that this kind of solution appeals to me more. (Glowacki, 1990)

We turn now to *Social Breakdown* in the conversational discourse.

SOCIAL BREAKDOWN IN THE DISCUSSIONS

Figure 4.2 compares the performances of *Social Breakdown* and *Faulty System* in the peer group discussions. The chart indicates that *Social Breakdown's* performance was even stronger than that of *Faulty System:* 60% of the groups unanimously embraced its claims; none unanimously rejected them.

As Figure 4.3 indicates, the frame's overall performance was strong in both black and white groups, but its contents were more likely to be contested in the latter than the former. How this was so will be discussed at the end of the chapter, in the section on frame rebuttals.

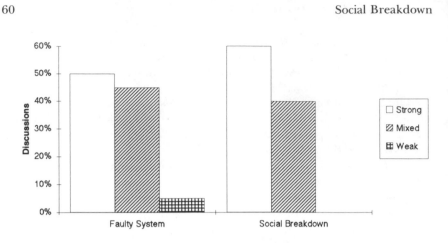

Figure 4.2. Faulty System and Social Breakdown in the discussions.

Three additional factors attest to the overall strength of *Social Break-down's* performance: First, participants in almost every group responded to the frame's trigger statement enthusiastically, often interrupting its reading to signal approval. Second, in the eight discussions in which the frame was contested, the voices raised against it were always in the minority and typically offered only tepid objections to this or that aspect of the frame while acceding to its core claims. Third, in terms of sheer volume, discourse expressing *Social Breakdown* commanded roughly *twice* as much space in the transcripts as discourse expressing either *Blocked Opportunities* or *Faulty System.*

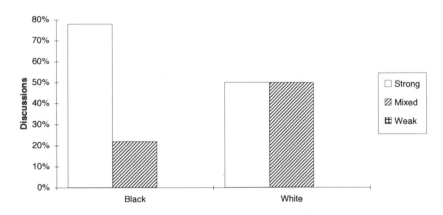

Figure 4.3. Social Breakdown in the discussions, by race.

SUPPORTIVE ARGUMENTS

How did discussion participants conjure *Social Breakdown?* How does their discourse compare with the discourse of the op ed writers? We will examine five lines of argument, each propounded by group members in more than one discussion. The first of these consists of general claims concerning a putative crisis in values or morality. The next four correspond, in a general way, to the four categories of display examined in the previous section in relation to the public discourse.

Value Crisis

Participants in 17 groups (85%) conjured *Social Breakdown* by alleging that society is in the midst of some sort of general crisis of values or morality. Claims extended from the general assertion that "all the traditional values are lost" to particular laments concerning diminishing respect for elders, waning authority, and declining "family values," religion and personal responsibility. One woman expressed concern over the distribution of condoms in schools (in fact, she expressed concern about "condos"—but the slump in Boston real estate was not what she had in mind). Unfortunately, there is no neat way to summarize these wide ranging sentiments other than to point out that they share in common the notion that values and morality "ain't what they used to be." The series of five brief excerpts that follow were selected to capture the diversity of these sentiments, if not to represent them in an exhaustive fashion:

1

Group: **Woodman Road**

Doris: Yeah, I think the whole of society—not just this neighborhood—needs to return to a moral, traditional standard. Parents as well as children, all across the board—from the poor neighborhood to the rich neighborhood, whatever, needs to return to morals, good old fashioned morals. The Bible.

2

Group: **Gordon Road**

Sally: But I mean it's the discipline. You can't—

Martha:	Traditional rites and mores.
Edward:	All the traditional values are lost—
Unknown:	Yes, that's correct.
Edward:	People are out to get what they can get for themselves.
Martha:	The ironic part of it is that the children themselves are suffering from it. They don't realize it. But they are suffering from it. Because they don't know where to turn or what to do. I mean they don't know "Am I doing right?" They say "Who cares? Who knows?" They don't know.

3

Group: Hallibut Square

Laura:	I think there's a total disintegration of any kind of—
Janet:	Morality.
Laura:	—morality and structure that helps people find some kind of, y'know, balance.

4

Group: Maple Street

Maynard:	But I think the big problem, in my mind, of why I'd say crime has got worse, and I think the reason for it has been authority. The authority symbol has waned in the home, it's waned in the church, it's waned in the schools. Given that, people get their own figures of authority, or else take authority into their own hands. . . . I think we have to get back to respect for authority. But authority has to earn their respect if they want to get them back.

5

Group: Fisher Hill Road

Deborah:	You have these kids that have no respect for anything. They have no values, no parameters. They are making babies because they don't have any. They can't teach their kids any. And the population is just growing to epidemic proportions, and these people are going to

take us to hell. I mean I know I sound like a preacher but it's true.

[brief clamor]

Lloyd: I went to this rap concert. The Departments? The last one we just had? I couldn't believe the girls there. Right. And you know they're saying swears.

Deborah: Oh yeah, filthy!

Lloyd: And repeat, the singers are saying repeat it. And the girls are out there, F this, F that, whatever—I'm looking at these young girls, and I'm saying, what are they doing?

Chuck: A lot of the lyrics was downing women.

Lloyd: They don't even understand what they're doing. And they're up there, yeah, you know—

Unknown: Yeah, I can't cuss in front of my mom and daddy now!

Deborah: I know it. You know it. You wouldn't dare—Out of respect.

Interestingly, in the School Street group several participants conjured *Social Breakdown* to counter the suggestion that the prohibition on drugs be lifted. Consider the following excerpt:

Cast:

Betty, a retiree and high school graduate, white, in her mid 70s.
Frances, a school teacher with a graduate degree, African American, in her mid 50s.
Janice, an assistant treasurer and high school graduate, African American, in her mid 40s.

Betty: Maybe they've got to legalize drugs?

Frances: That wouldn't solve anything.

Unknown: That would get rid of the drug dealers.

Janice: But then we have—what we forget—is that it was legalized at one time.

Unknown: But they'll still mug you to get the money to go buy the drugs.

[laughter]

Betty: So it wouldn't be so expensive, they wouldn't be making that kind of money.

Frances: I think that's why we're in the situation we are now, because we keep relaxing the rules—

Janice: Exactly.
Frances: —to fit the people, and you can't—You have to enforce it.
Janice: There has to be a bottom line.
Betty: They're just going to keep on killing people.

[A few paragraphs further down in the transcript:]

Janice: But this is part of it. It's church, schools, home, no one's doing their job. That's why it is. It used to that—church used to play a big part in the family. Your family did. Your friends. If you were out here acting up, you didn't want anybody to know it. Now you brag about it because you're not taught any values at home. And if you're not taught—if it doesn't start at home, the street's got you. The street has you. And you've a school system that is rigged against you. They keep relaxing the laws and this—I'm with Frances—do not relax the laws. Do not relax the standards. It does not help. It makes it worse. If a child knows that he or she can come in that classroom at 11:00 in the morning—O.K. half the school day is over—and still get marked present, be disruptive, beat up teachers and still not get thrown out—and other folks see it—what are you going to do?

In Frances' and Janice's discourse, crime stems not from absence of economic opportunity, for example, but from the failure of "church, schools and home" to "do their job"—that is, to instill values and impose standards of conduct. The prospect of legal drug use is repellent to these women because it implies a further erosion of public expectations concerning values and conduct. In Frances' words, "that's why we're in the situation we are now, because we keep relaxing the rules."

Negligent Parenting

In the op ed sample, attributions for crime to what criminologists Eleanor and Sheldon Glueck once referred to as "under-the-roof culture" (Currie, 1985) were rare, appearing in just three of the op eds (5%). In nearly all of the discussions, however, participants insisted that crime stems from the failure of parents to supervise, discipline and properly care for their children. More specifically, attributions of this sort were expressed in *all* of the black and mixed groups and in six of the eight white groups. These sentiments were communicated both as bald assertions and through the telling of personal experience narratives that contrasted prevailing child-rearing practices with participants' memories of their own upbringings. As an example of the latter, consider the following excerpt from a lengthy speech by Vanessa, whom we first met in the previous chapter (see p. 51):

Group: Troy Street

Vanessa: I think that there is a lot of responsibility on parents. And I think that when you say that as a black person, people are like "Blaming the victim." Well I'm sorry, you have to raise your children. You *have* to raise your children to be responsible, to act responsibly and to value people and to value life and to value people's property. If you don't do that you are lacking as a parent. And again you can't always control how your children come out, but I've seen it again and again where people don't even make the effort. And I think that as a community we need to take that back. As parents, we need to make demands of our children. We need to discipline our children and make them know what's what. I mean there's good and there's bad, to me, and I make sure my daughter knows, there's black and white, and there's good and bad, and never mind this fuzzy gray line. She'll figure that out as an adult. But for a five-year-old mind you have to say good and bad, moral, immoral. That's the only way children learn about what's right and how to be good people. And I think my mother instilled that in me. I think as a community, particularly in the black community, we have to say that. Parents, you have to control your children. You *have* to. We are lacking that strongly, as parents, to a large extent. We do not control our children, to a large extent. . . . There's no doubt that it can be done. I am a product of very poor parents. We were never on welfare and my parents were always together, but were always lower class. I think Michael's the same and maybe others in here. There are people that do it in spite of the system. You can do it. You have to have parents that instill in you the fact that it can be done. You have to want to do it. If you're a black person there's no doubt that there's racism, that it's rampant. You can overcome it and that's what you have to teach your children. There's gonna be times when it's gonna overcome you. In

the long run you can overcome it. I think we really have
to work together.

There will be racism and other obstacles, Vanessa is saying, but children
raised by diligent parents can overcome them. Unfortunately, too many
parents are failing in their duty to teach their children to "value
people . . . life . . . and people's property."

A second example of discourse critical of prevailing child-rearing
practices comes from the Main Street group. This excerpt also features a
general lament concerning contemporary values, and several tropes typical of other *Social Breakdown* displays. We will have occasion to refer back
to it in the sections that follow:

Cast:

Ben, a building and grounds supervisor with more than a college degree,
African American, in his early 60s.
Helen, a retiree and high school graduate, African American, in her
mid 70s.
Gloria, a bookkeeper and high school graduate, African American, in her
late 50s.
Sarah, a retiree from Cape Verdean, who did not complete high school, in
her early 60s.

Gloria: I feel as though it's happening because of the homes
          that some of these young people may come out of.
          Lack of supervision, lack of parents—parents being
          parents.
Ben: No guidance. [Right—a voice interjects] A few years
          back on TV, you remember, "It's 11:00 o'clock, do
          you know where your children are?" And the answer
          to that today is "Yeah, they're outside on the street
          somewhere."
Gloria: No commitment in the home, no commitment in
          schools. Parents do not go to parent/teachers' meet-
          ings. They don't go to the schools until the student has
          a real serious problem.
Ben: And then they get angry with the teacher.
Gloria: Yes. Or angry with the principal, or angry with the
          guidance counselor, or angry with the bus drivers. It's
          everybody else's fault.
Ben: There is no respect.

Unknown: Oh, we know that.
    Ben: They don't respect themselves. They don't respect anyone else. When I was young I was taught *that* was one of the keys to everything. I hate to sound like Rodney Dangerfield—But I don't get no respect!
  Gloria: It goes back also to parents not going to church themselves so the children do not go. And there's certain guidance they receive when they go to church and Sunday school. The children are just not doing these things anymore. Parents are not requiring it or demanding it because they don't do it themselves.
    Ben: [Turning to the facilitator:] Do you call your mother by her first name?
Facilitator: No. Of course not.
    Ben: Neither do I. And I'm quite a bit older than you are.
   Helen: Do you hear that now, youngsters calling their mothers—
    Ben: Oh yes. They'd call their fathers by their first name if they could *find* some of them. That's one of those things—
  Gloria: It's the time we're living in, you know. Things have really changed.
    Ben: But it shouldn't be.
  Gloria: But it's there. Can we turn it around?

In Gloria's view, young people become involved in crime because their parents lack the level of commitment necessary for proper child-rearing. This lack of commitment is in evidence when parents fail to attend church and to visit their children's schools. As far as Ben is concerned, it is also in evidence when children disrespect their elders. Properly reared children know better.

Discourse charging parents with responsibility for crime was richer and more expansive in the discussions of the black groups; there were more attributions to poor parenting, on average, within the black discussions, and speakers making such attributions contributed more in terms of transcript lines. Nevertheless, similar discourse could also be heard in three quarters of the white discussions. In the excerpt that follows, two white school teachers compare notes on their pupils' parents.

Group: Maple Street
Cast:

Melissa, a teacher with a graduate degree, in her early 40s.
Eve, a teacher with a graduate degree, in her early 60s.

Melissa: I don't know about you Eve but I see that parents can't set limits for their kids. They can't. If you sit down with them in a conference and you say, you know, I notice that your child really has some difficulty accepting limits—this is what I'm trying to do. They have no idea what to do. And if I say to them, "Well you could try having consequences for their behavior—you know—like—pick something." And so some will say, "Well, he swears." So I say, "Well, O.K., if he swears, then he needs to have something that's going to happen when he does that, like maybe send him to his room." And they'll look at me and say, "But he'll cry."

Eve: Yes.

Stella: Yes.

Melissa: It's like [they] just don't understand it.

Eve: Exactly.

Melissa: And you've got to lay down the law, so to speak, and it doesn't have to be harsh, but it's got to be steady and consistent, and I just don't think that we're doing it.

Eve: No.

Melissa: They don't. They don't stick to their guns.

Parents, the teachers are saying, no longer understand the necessity of establishing and enforcing clear rules of conduct. In a sense, they have given up the fight, preferring to keep their children happy (and quiet) rather than imposing discipline.

One feature of discourse critical of prevailing parenting practices deserves special attention because of its frequent occurrence. The conversationalists in half of the groups charged that parents, when confronted with the delicts of their children, deny the message and assail the messenger. We have already seen an example of this trope, in the excerpt from the discussion of the Main Street group, quoted above. In that discussion, Ben claimed that when told of their children's difficulties in school, parents "get angry with the teachers." Gloria responded "Or angry with the principal, or angry with the guidance counselor," and so on. Details varied slightly across the discussions—sometimes the complaining agent is a teacher, other times a neighbor—but the central claim that parents deny the message and assail the messenger is always the same.

In six of the ten discussions featuring this charge, speakers integrated a personal experience narrative, explaining that in the past parents would "back up" teachers or neighbors who complained about their child whereas today they are more apt to "jump down their throats."

Two examples of this type of claim follow. The speaker in the first is Beatrice, an African American woman who works as a quality control inspector. She is in her mid 50s.

Group: Woodman Road

Beatrice: And my thing about the neighbors—I truly honestly believe if it was like it were when I was kid, things would be much better. It would be much better. If a neighbor could speak to your child and to my child and tell that child—And if that child got unruly, you put a switch on that child and send him home, or you put that kid on punishment, that child would be much better. But now nobody wants you to touch their kid. Their kids don't do this. Their kids don't do that, O.K.? And it's not only just in this little area. It's all over. And it's *bad*. It's really bad. I can say one thing, I haven't had any problems with [our neighborhood] kids because . . . they are good. I mean I speak to these kids. They may not like it. They may go off and mumble, but I haven't had no problems. But I hear other neighbors say: "This kid there cussed me out. This kid do this." I tell anybody, if your kid cusses me, I'm gonna slap, you know? I mean you might have to sit down and talk about it after—say, well you tell me to do this, do that. But I'll be doggone if I'm gonna be a Mama or Grandma and have to come to you, "You're child cussed me." It don't make sense. I'm the oldest. I should be able to tell your kid, "You don't talk that way. You gonna talk that way, you go into that house." O.K.? Because I'm not gonna hurt your child no more that I would hurt—I'd probably hurt mine quicker than I'd hurt yours. But they just—You can't say nothing to these kids because everybody is in an uproar. "You don't say this to my kid." It should be each member of this area could be able to speak to somebody's kids and it wouldn't be no hardships.

When Beatrice was young, neighbors could correct a mischievous child without fear of incurring the wrath of his parents. But these days, "everybody is in an uproar."

For Alex, the television producer introduced in the introduction, the situation is much the same. But in his version of the trope, parents of the mischievous child are not satisfied to merely make a fuss:

Group: Jacob's Lane

Alex: The teachers aren't allowed to discipline too. And I hate this phrase more than anything in the world and that is, "when I was a kid." When I was kid if you got in trouble in school, you better not go home and say you were in trouble in school because you'll get in trouble at home. Nowadays you go home and say you're in trouble in school, the parent asks what it was. "Let's go down and sue the teachers for getting you into trouble."

In most of the discussions, participants, at least implicitly, offered one or more explanations for the poor state of parental guidance and supervision. We encountered one such explanation already, when Gloria (above, in this section) insisted that "it goes back . . . to parents not going to church themselves so the children do not go." We can now be a bit more systematic: In all, participants argued that poor parenting is due to family breakdown or the absence of fathers (11 groups); selfishness and greed—especially with respect to parents who tolerate drug trafficking in order to benefit from its fruits (5 groups); the need to work in order to make ends meet (6 groups); the youthfulness of so many parents due to "babies having babies" (4 groups); substance abuse (4 groups); and the intrusion of government into family life through laws governing child abuse (6 groups).

The last item deserves elaboration. In five black groups and one white, participants argued, sometimes repeatedly, that laws against child abuse discourage or prevent parents, teachers and neighbors from disciplining children. Their logic? In one participant's words: "Since the courts have said child abuse these children know how far they can go, and how far *you* can go." The racial differences for this claim are striking, especially in light of the fact that it was sharply contested in the white discussion but apparently accepted as a common place in the black ones. In the extended illustration that follows, Sam tells of a 13-year-old removed from his home by the state, and Karl shares an experience that demonstrates his unwillingness to cede what he feels are his parental rights and obligations.

Group: Fisher Hill
Cast: (See p. 25)
New Addition:

Sam, a retiree and high school graduate, in his 70s.

Sam: You know it's a lot different now then when we were coming up. Because I know when I was coming up, if I did something wrong, was bad, it didn't have to be no one in my family. The woman down the street would get me and whip my behind and sent me home and I'd get a licking when I git there. And you know I know some people right here in Boston now, that the State is trying to take this kid now, because they spanked this kid. The kid is 13-years-old. He went to school and said his mother whupped him with a belt. Then they took that kid out of school!

Karl: Well you know what I'd do? Look, I tell them, you take him and raise him.

Sam: I'm just telling you. So when they go to school and the teacher tells them things, they talk back to the teacher, they say what they want to say, and then they come home, you can't whup them, you know.

Georgia: And that's what Lloyd was saying before about being too liberal.

Sam: Right, that's right!

[clamor]

Chuck: There's no respect.

Karl: You know what I did? The little one, we're back on the little one again. When that law first come out she was about 13 or 14, the little one: "You can't whup me, I'll call the police." Shit my hair rolled upon my head. I took my belt, whupped the ass, drove up to the phone and said "You call the policeman." And I had made up my mind if he come near talking about me, put me in jail, I said "Look you put me in jail, now you take her and take care. Don't bring her back here when I get out of jail. I don't want to catch her back here. Because I'm not going to kill my kid." See I ain't gonna let the police officer tell me how to raise my kid. See people just making excuses, not doing what they're supposed to do. If we take care of them kids while they're young—I ain't never whupped her since.

In Karl's view, his daughter needed to be whupped, as evidenced by the fact that she never again misbehaved in a similar fashion. To the extent that police and state social service agencies discourage corporal punishment, these African American men are saying, they discourage parents from properly disciplining their children.

Community Breakdown

In 14 discussions (70%), participants conjured the frame by attributing crime, at least in part, to a breakdown in community. Race differences are noteworthy with respect to both the content and quantity of this discourse, so we shall consider the white and black groups separately.

Discourse on the degraded quality of community life could be heard in five white groups but was typically offered in only brief utterances. In three groups speakers simply observed that these days "people don't know their neighbors." In one white group, a participant remembered that in the past, "if I was going out shopping . . . somebody always took care of our kids. The kids were everybody's kids—they weren't your kids or her kids." And in another a participant recalled that "years ago if you spit on the sidewalk your parents would get 15 phonecalls."

In the black groups discourse on degraded neighborliness was typically much richer. Speakers frequently contrasted prevailing neighboring practices with those remembered from their childhoods. We already know from our review of discourse on parenting practices that in the past parents "whupped" their children whenever neighbors complained about their behavior. In this section we see that in the past, neighbors also did their share of whupping. In all seven of the black groups that conjured the frame through discourse on degraded neighborliness, speakers recalled that in their childhood communities neighbors enjoyed "spanking rights" (the frame was also conjured in this fashion in one mixed group by an African American participant). For some group members this meant that as children, whenever they were caught misbehaving, they got a "double whammy." Sam's speech from the excerpt quoted above contains an instance of this trope. Another could be heard in the discussion of the Longwood Road group:

Cast:

Martin, a firefighter and high school graduate, in his mid 30s.
Marjory, a teacher with a graduate degree, in her early 30s.

> Martin: When I was growing up, it was like, if some parent seen me doing something wrong, it was like "open season on Martie." They could smack you upside the head, and it was O.K., and then they'll tell your father, and you go get it again when he comes home. So it was like—
>
> Marjory: A double whammy!
>
> Martin: Yeah.

> *Marjory:*   And you got it twice as hard because you now embar-
>   rassed your mother.
> *Unknown:*   And disrespected an adult!

In three black and one mixed group, African American speakers also insisted that in their childhood communities neighbors were more help-ful than they are today. While supervision and care of children was the form of help most commonly mentioned, Michael, an African American participant in the discussion of the Troy Street group, told of another type of neighborly assistance. Michael is a college graduate in his mid 30s and works for a state agency as an economist:

> *Michael:*   I'll chime in. I grew up in a neighborhood—what I'll call
>   a real neighborhood. And I grew up very poor. But one
>   thing about growing up as poor as I did is that we had a
>   sense of community. And we really had to work as a
>   community, because individually the people of the com-
>   munity could not have survived by themselves. The only
>   way that we could survive is that we had to pull together
>   as a community. An example of that is that we were
>   constantly without food. I did not eat every day. What we
>   do sometimes is we would go around to the various
>   neighbors, I need a cup of flour, I need a cup of milk. Go
>   tell Ms. Sue to send me some baking powder and salt.
>   And we would borrow amongst ourselves in order to
>   make that bread. Children just got together and played.
>   This is one thing that—children today, I come in the
>   neighborhood and say "where are the children?" [In my]
>   day you see like tons of children. We just played together
>   as big groups of children when I was growing up. And
>   there was spanking rights throughout the neighborhood
>   and this type of thing. And I long for that.

How do the participants explain the breakdown in community about which they speak? For the most part, they do not. Community atomiza-tion and the degradation of neighborliness are *described,* but not *ex-plained,* much as one might describe the experience of growing old without feeling any need to explain the biological determinants of aging. But the transcripts do suggest two possible explanations, one or the other of which is implicit in the discourse of five of the black groups. First, in three discussions participants explained their own or others' reluctance to intervene to correct a mischievous child by pointing out the increasing likelihood that the child's parent will react in a hostile fashion. We encountered discourse on this general theme above, in the section on parenting practices.

The second implicit explanation for community breakdown highlights the "random" nature of street violence and the apparent unpredictability of its youthful perpetrators. In three discussions speakers commented that nowadays they must think twice before intervening to correct a child. The following excerpt from the Longwood Road group is typical. The speaker is Charles, a mental health worker in his late 20s.

> *Charles:* I mean, I myself, I keep my values. And if I see a kid on this street doing something, if I know who he is, I'm gonna tell him to his face. Because I guess I'm willing to take a risk. But if I'm going down to Castlegate [a housing project], and if I see some kid, a five-year old—If I see a 10-year-old kid, you know, stealing a tire off a car, I might mention something, but believe me I'm not gonna say *hey what y*—I'm not gonna grab him. I'll say—I might go "is that your car?" But I keep walking. I won't—I'm more intent to mind my business than I will to intervene in something of that nature—You know, somewhere else. Because I like my life, you know?

Charles tries to keep his values, but in a reputedly tough section of town even he is unwilling to risk direct intervention to stop a delinquent child.

Recreational Activities

If conversationalists assert that crime stems from an erosion in the capacity of families and communities to regulate their members' conduct, then we might expect them to favor crime control strategies that seek to enhance informal social controls. This expectation is amply confirmed through the participants' persistent advocacy in 15 discussions (75%) of structured programs and supervised gathering places for urban young people. Among the interventions most commonly suggested were recreational activities, after-school programs, youth centers, mentor programs, organized sports and staffed parks. Race differences were not apparent with respect to the popularity of these ideas.

Many participants were quite specific in explaining the anticrime rationale behind the interventions they proposed. For example, Sandy, a bank executive with a college degree, offered the following account in response to the statement used to trigger the frame *Blocked Opportunities:*

Group: Meadowbrook Street

Sandy: When you talk about education and family values and all
that sort of thing, it's giving people options—it's—there
are some very [good] programs in terms of when you challenge the kids and when you get them involved in art
programs and sports programs and you basically get them
using their time in more of a constructive fashion they
don't have as much time to basically sit around and feel
bored and look for trouble to get into. I think we've all
been there as kids ourselves and if that's what they're advocating then I'm all for it. I think that would help, definitely,
in terms of reducing the crime. And also, it's not only
going to do it because you're keeping the kids busy, but it's
also because you're teaching them good value systems at
the same time.

We should also note that a good deal of the advocacy of "education"
and "job creation" stressed their centrality as mechanisms for informal
social control rather than as means for earning money and moving up
the class ladder. Where an utterance clearly and unequivocally treated
job creation or education as strategies for enhancing moral and inter-
personal integration rather than for ameliorating poverty or relative
deprivation, it was coded as displaying *Social Breakdown* (where ambi-
guity existed with respect to the speaker's intention, the utterance was
coded as an expression of *Blocked Opportunities*). For example, in the
discussion of the Woodman Road group, Beatrice argues that there
should be "more jobs" for young people in order to "keep their minds
occupied to do something . . . to keep them busy." Because this utterance treats jobs strictly as a means for integrating young people into
conventional behavior, it was coded as displaying *Social Breakdown*.

In stressing the importance of "keeping kids busy" speakers in two
groups wielded the maxim "idle hands are the devil's workshop." While
conversationalists in the other groups neglected the maxim, most would
surely have agreed with its message. Indeed, in nine groups (45%) participants commented that young people have either "no place to go" or
"nothing to do." Consider the following illustration:

Group: Hallibut Square
Cast: (See p. 46)

Phyllis: I think that especially during the summertime that our
parks should be staffed. We should have someplace for
kids to go—something for them to do. Definitely. And I

don't mean just for the poor and disadvantaged, quote
unquote. But for every kid, everybody to be able to have a
place to go and something to do.

Janet: That is one thing we did have as kids.

Bob: Yeah.

Janet: We did have the park—

Phyllis: And we had the gym—mine had the gym and the park.
Mine were fortunate to have both places. Kids today don't
have either place.

The Hallibut Square group members acknowledge that as kids, whatever
deprivations they endured, they always had the park and the gym. In
contrast, young people today seem to have no place to go, and this strikes
the group members as part of the problem.

Anticrime Activism

It is hardly surprising that participants in 16 groups (80%) offered
spontaneous support for anticrime activities such as crime watch. While
discourse of this sort conjures the frame, it is clearly related to the fact
that the setting for each discussion was a neighborhood crime watch
meeting. As it happens, however, the frame's overall performance (see
p. 60) would be unchanged if all references to crime watch were excluded from analysis. Bearing this in mind, we turn now to keyings of
the frame through discourse on citizen anticrime activism.

Participants offered three distinct defenses of anticrime activism.
First, in seven groups they argued that watchful neighbors deter a good
deal of crime, in particular burglaries and muggings. The excerpt that
follows is a particularly colorful explanation of the logic of crime watch
as understood by most participants. We have already met Henry, the
African American police officer quoted in Chapter 3. The new speaker
is Henry's wife Ruth, an African American graduate student in her 40s:

Group: Grove Hills Parkway

Henry: I got involved and I really care about it because I see that
the police can only go so far. I mean I sit right here [and]
I've been awakened in the middle of the night where a cab
driver's been shot right outside my bedroom window. My
neighbor's son was killed right here in front of my house. I
called for help because there's fights right out—I've seen
my neighbors get robbed there. All my neighbors have
been robbed. Mr. Ferraro was knocked down this hill. His

wrist was broken—an old man. And then Mr. Wilson was robbed and Mr. Smith was robbed right here in front of my neighbor Johnson's house. Guys have been going into the windows of my neighbors while they're home at night. People who used to live across the street. And they got the hell out because they were scared. . . . . The police are out there somewhere and if someone contacts, communicates, then police come. [But] by that time the guy has done what the hell he wants—the criminal has done what the hell he wants to do and he's made off. Crime watch is people. When she [indicating Ruth] gets out of the car . . . she beeps her horn, another neighbor can look out the window, come out on the porch because at certain hours of the evening that's when everyone, these women, are getting ripped off. There's somebody that looks and once in a while they come and they start snatching. When they get out of their car the guy will just jump out of nowhere. He'll pretend like he's going up on the porch, like other people in the neighborhood, and when she gets walking up her steps, he sneaks up behind and grabs her and grabs her bag and takes off. If neighbors look out the window—or somebody—I'll walk out on my porch—you hear somebody's blowing the horn—come out and stand out there and this guy who's gonna try to rip her off, he gonna see me standing there saying "How you doing Sally." And I'll look at him. And another time a guy come down and he sneak in and he stands at my corner. I was in my room. I was typing on the computer. And I look out my window, and he's been peeking way down my street and he goes over the other part and comes back up and—now this is neighborhood crime watch now in effect—I says, "Hey asshole, what are you looking for?" "I was just going to my girlfriends." "Why don't you go home and say something to her? What's her name? Get the hell out of here or I'll call the cops." That's crime watch there, that's what happens. That's why I got involved, you know.

Ruth: That's the most excellent point that was made. That is crime watch in action. That is *in action.* To me it's like a watering hole. You know you have a watering hole and all the animals in the jungle come to the watering hole, the lions, the tigers and the folks that they eat. Well that's what this street is like at night. You got criminals. They're thinking about how can I rob you and you look at them saying now how can I get in the house before you rob me. And unless another lion comes along and says *roar* [makes sound], then you're going to get mugged. It is just like that out here at night.

Note that even speeches that stress the practical utility of crime watch have a rich moral tenor. In Chapter 2 we learned that participants typically insisted that they were not really fearful of losing their property as much as the possibility of being hurt, or of having a loved one or neighbor hurt. Here, in Henry and Ruth's discourse on the practical utility of crime watch, we see the expression of a similar *moral* concern with protecting loved ones and neighbors from harm.

Second, participants in two groups also argued that crime watch can be an effective means of extracting services and improved police protection from the state. The crime watch group can serve as a mechanism for "holding politicians accountable" the speakers argued.

Finally, conversationalists in nine groups (45%) discussed crime watch as, at least in part, a means of fostering community solidarity and reconstituting the neighborhood "as it used to be." Their discourse is sometimes reminiscent of Durkheim's (1964) argument that crime serves a positive function for society in so far as it causes people to band together to punish offenders and thereby ritually affirm the prevailing moral order. Consider the following two examples, the first from the Jacob's Lane group.

Cast: (See p. 41)
New Addition:

Paula, a fundraiser for a nonprofit organization with more than a college degree, in her mid 40s.

> Paula: Even things like the crime watch gatherings we've had
> —you know, kind of the parties for kids and the block
> parties. That is like an old-fashioned thing.
>
> Geraldine: I think that's really like an extension of the family [several voices echo sentiment].
>
> Peg: If neighborhoods pull together in the way that they [used to] naturally come together—
>
> Laura: *Naturally* come together. So we have to *force* it now to come together.

The next example is from the Troy Street group. We have already met Michael (p. 73) and Vanessa (p. 51). The new cast member is Ronnie, a college graduate who works in human resources. She is white and in her mid 30s. The group is responding to the question "Why did you get involved in crime watch and what do you hope to accomplish?"

> *Ronnie:* I really believe that the way the society affects people is that we get very isolated, we get divided and we end up throwing grenades at each other, either mentally or physically. . . . And so I feel compelled to try to figure out, to whatever degree I can, to bring people together. . . .
>
> *Michael:* I guess my ideal thing would be to bring back Halloween the way I remember. I mean, that is such a lost tradition as well as piece of our society. Halloween was such a fun time. I mean you would just take and you wouldn't have to worry about whether this person going to snatch you and take you away. And you could just roam for miles throughout the community collecting. Now mom and dad have to take you from house to house. And before you can eat the candy you have to take it to some place and stand in line and have it X rayed. I don't want the damn candy now. That's no fun!
>
> *Facilitator:* People X ray candy? Do people really X ray candy?
>
> *Michael:* Oh yeah. They take it to the hospital and they X ray it. How can they have a good time—spoil the whole thing. What are you going to say to the child? You can't trust. You can't trust.
>
> *Vanessa:* And the sad fact is, you can't. That's the saddest part! You really can't.
>
> *Michael:* Bring back Halloween the way it was.

When this final line of argument—that crime watch is a means of fostering community solidarity—is considered in relation to the overall strong performance of *Social Breakdown,* an interesting possibility emerges: Participating in a crime watch groups may be, for many group members, not merely a strategy for increasing personal safety and protecting investments in homes and property (though it is certainly that), but also a means of addressing what they believe to be the *root cause* of crime, namely, apathy, urban anonymity, and self-interested pursuit of personal advantage at the expense of community. In other words, participation in crime watch may be, for many participants, primarily a *moral gesture.* Let me make this idea as clear as possible: If one believes that crime stems from poverty, then antipoverty programs are indicated; if one believes that crime stems from a poorly functioning criminal justice system, then reform of that system is in order; but if one believes that crime stems from a crisis in values and morality, what then? For the conversationalists, participation in neighborhood-based collective action, in so far as it expresses altruistic concern for the well being of others, may be as much a "root cause-solution" as tougher law enforcement or better jobs programs. Of course, motivations are elusive phenomena; it is hard enough to recognize one's own let alone those of others. But the moral tone of so much of the discourse on crime watch seems to support this hypothesis. And at least one participant made the connection explicit, albeit in a slightly jumbled statement. The speaker is Jenny, a college graduate who works as a project controls engineer. She is explaining her decision to participate in a street patrol organized by her upscale neighborhood group.

Group: Meadowbrook Street

Jenny: I think that it's that sense of making a better community, not so much that I think I can cure—I don't do it to solve crimes. I do it for the benefit of the community spirit type of thing. And I think that the problem—I mean I'll go back to my moral fiber speech again [laughter]. I think that the problem is that people don't have a sense of helping a community and doing whatever it's gonna take to help it and to become a part of a community and that they have an obligation to do that. That they're not gonna be able to pay somebody else to patrol the street for them. And I've had neighbors come up and complain about being accosted on the street. And you say well this is what you could do to help. And they're like, well can't I just give $500 a year and hire somebody to do it? Well no you can't because you're not going to get that same overall feeling for everything, you know? Can't we just hire somebody to sweep the street so I don't have to? It's that whole sense of what you're responsible—what you have to do to be a responsible member of your community. And that's what's missing.

Jenny became active in anticrime activities not to "solve crimes," but to "make the community better." In her earlier "moral fiber speech" (excerpted as the epigram to this chapter) she attributed crime to the "breakdown" of society's "moral structure," arguing that people no longer feel that "they have to nurture their neighbor." In the present speech, she again asserts that "what's missing"—and presumably at the heart of the crime problem—is altruism and civic responsibility. She seems to be saying that by acting as a good neighbor and model citizen, she is addressing the essence of the disease that manifests itself in crime, rather than merely battling its symptoms.[3]

Liberal and Conservative Inflections

Discourse inflecting *Social Breakdown* in a conservative fashion was absent from the op ed sample but clearly present in the peer group discussions. The clearest traces of a conservative accent could be heard in discourse on child-rearing, especially in the black groups. In charging that child abuse laws have undermined parental authority, participants echoed general conservative criticisms of intrusive government and "elitist" social workers. Other traces of a conservative accent could be heard in two white groups in which participants charged, albeit a bit elliptically, that crime is rooted in the culture of the social movements of the 1960s and 1970s. In reaction to a story about a school principal who interfered with an effort to punish a child for repeatedly "hooking" school, for example, one speaker explained that, "It's this movement of like free to do what you want whether that gets in somebody else's way or not—that's right because it pleases me."

Liberal inflections of the frame could be heard in four discussions. As in the public discourse, these consisted of utterances that conflated *Blocked Opportunities* and *Social Breakdown*, typically arguing either that unemployment is a source of family and community disintegration, or that job creation is necessary to help keep families together and thereby reduce crime. The following exchange between Henry and Ruth is illustrative:

Group: Grove Hills Parkway
Cast: (See p. 76)

 Ruth: [T]ake some of the middle-class, upper-middle class folks, from wherever they come from—suburbs, whatever—and take away their job for a month, O.K.? Where they don't get their paycheck. And see what starts to happen in their family. You know that to me answers a lot of questions . . .

[A few paragraphs down in the transcript:]

 Henry: The best way to fight crime is . . . teaching the family to take responsibility more in bringing up the kids, providing the jobs for the family people, promoting family again . . . *jobs*, doing what you can to give support to that family.

REBUTTAL ARGUMENTS

One or another element of *Social Breakdown* was rejected in eight discussions (40%). Participants in four groups argued that most children raised in single parent families do just fine, so single parenthood per se should not be regarded as a cause of crime. Participants in three groups argued that some kids wind up criminals in spite of their parents best efforts, therefore crime must be regarded as a matter of personal *choice*.

In addition to these rebuttal arguments, participants in seven groups expressed reservations about the notion that either "family breakdown" or "family values" is a source of crime. These speakers were apparently aware that in the public discourse the family breakdown argument is increasingly associated with a conservative or traditionalist political position, a position with which they were uncomfortable being associated. One example of this type of rebuttal appears as Vanessa's contribution to the epigram for this chapter. Another was delivered by Margaret whom we first met in Chapter 3 (see p. 40).

Group: Peach Tree Lane

Margaret: You know when Vice-President Quayle said that we don't have family values . . . . I think we can have family values without having family *neatness*. Know what I mean? Now for instance you take a 16-year-old girl who *wants* to be pregnant. Wants to be pregnant because she has a mother that's indifferent, she has a father that's indifferent, she has brothers that are indifferent. This baby will be *hers*. There are children like that. [I've heard 'em say it—a voice interjects] They are *children* but they want a child—those little fingers to wrap around theirs. That little smile, you know, in the middle of the night. And that [makes a polite version of a burping noise]. You know how babies just turn them on! And they want that love. So this is the single mother— they have no family values? I don't really understand how they can't see the nature of things. But they're Republicans of course [laughter]. Republicans, they're like ice—*Ice Man Commeth*. That's the way I feel about Republicans . . . . They form this icicle around them. They don't see past Ozzie Nelson and whatever the name of his wife was and their two little children.

Ertha: Ozzie and Harriet.

Although the foregoing example is from an African American woman, discourse critical of the notion that "family breakdown" and "family values" are at the heart of the crime problem was more common in the white groups. In fact, it is *only* because such misgivings were expressed in five white groups but in just one black that the frame's overall performance was more frequently "mixed" in the former than in the latter (see Figure 4.3, p. 60).

Finally, it must be noted that even the speakers who leveled the criticisms described in this section typically expressed support for at least *some* of the frame's core claims. As an example of the tentative and partial nature of *Social Breakdown* rebuttals, consider one participant's response to the statement used to trigger the frame. Ellen is a white graduate student in her late 20s:

Group: Holyoke Street

Ellen: I somewhat disagree—agree [laughter]. I mean I think that all this stuff about the dissolution of the family is questionable as to whether that has actually happened. And there are a lot of single parent families and there are a lot of melded families and that kind of stuff throughout history. Maybe not in the fifties but there were other than in the fifties. There's been plenty of that and I don't think that the situation is the same. But on the other hand I do feel like you can take some control of the situation if neighbors know each other and act together. . . . I don't think it's a breakdown of the family but it just seems that it's a breakdown of people knowing their neighbors, knowing their communities, being just aware when people that don't live on the street, that might cause problems are even there. And that's a kind of cooperation that I think solves the problem.

Ellen rejects the notion that family breakdown is a source of crime; in the past, families of various configurations were quite common and thus all of the hullabaloo about single parent households rests on the false premise that they are something new. But even as Ellen rejects one element of the frame ("I don't think it's a breakdown of the family"), she embraces another ("it's a breakdown of people knowing their neighbors"). *Social Breakdown,* it seems, offers something for just about everyone.

CONCLUSION

Social Breakdown's performance in the op ed sample was not as strong a *Faulty System's.* The opposite proved true, however, in the peer group discussions. In fact, *Social Breakdown's* performance in the discussions was so strong that I have been tempted to label it a "consensus frame." This I have not done because members of several groups, as noted, expressed reservations about its claims concerning "family breakdown." Nevertheless, I can report that most elements of *Social Breakdown* were broadly resonant with virtually all of the discussion participants. Notably, even discourse absent in the op ed sample—on the failure of parents to discipline their kids and on the criminogenic effects of child abuse laws—proved important in the discussions.

In conjuring *Social Breakdown,* the discussion participants typically contrasted the prevailing normative order with one remembered from the past, and found the former lacking. The tenor of the frame's expressions, therefore, tended toward the nostalgic. Listening to the discussions, one learns that in the past parents disciplined their children and communities were tightly integrated. Today, neighborhoods are chaotic and authority is frequently absent. The conversationalists clearly sense a general breakdown of order and authority, a kind of societal unraveling. These feelings are all expressed in both white and black groups but perhaps, on the whole, with greater intensity and poignancy in the latter. We explore the existential and cultural sources of these feelings in Chapters 7–8.

What bearing does the evidence presented in this chapter have on the conventional wisdom about public opinion on crime? The best that we can say at this point is that it muddies the waters. *Social Breakdown* does not fit neatly into Stuart Scheingold's (1991) categories of "volitional" and "structural" criminology; it is not simply a "law and order" perspective of the sort described by Stuart Hall and his colleagues (1978), but neither does it attribute crime to capitalist political and economic relationships (cf. Elias, 1993). I will return to the question in Chapter 9, where I try to make sense of the political and public policy significance of popular consciousness about crime. Next we turn to popular discourse on the frame *Blocked Opportunities.*

NOTES

1.   Op eds advocating community policing were coded as displaying *Inefficiency,* and cross-coded as displaying *Social Breakdown* if they

stressed the idea of a "police-community partnership" or the role of regular people in fighting crime.

2.   See, for example, James Q. Wilson's *Thinking About Crime* (1983), or the many in-house publications on crime and the criminal justice system of the Heritage Foundation and the American Enterprise Institute (both in Washington, D.C.).

3.   If it is true that many participants view crime watch as a "root cause-solution" to crime, it does not necessarily follow that they are distinct from their neighbors in this regard. It is more likely that the quality of consciousness supportive of crime watch—i.e., *Social Breakdown*—is widespread among urban dwellers, but is insufficient in and of itself to engender participation. To fully explain the latter, we would need also to examine the nature of recruitment networks and state-sponsored crime prevention programs (cf. Lewis and Salem, 1986; on the relationship between consciousness and participation in collective action, see Gamson, 1992).

5

BLOCKED OPPORTUNITIES

A lot of young people are from homes where, you know, there isn't enough to eat and that sort of thing. I think that they're out roaming the streets and no one cares about them, and I think that if there were better living conditions and more opportunities for better education, I think that would help quite a bit.

Stella, a white woman in her mid 70s

I strongly disagree that there are not opportunities out there and this is why youth, or whoever, turn to crime. It's just that we're used to having our plate served to us. And when it's not served to us, then we get an attitude and we don't want to go find that plate. . . . Opportunities. That's the big word. Opportunity. That we don't have the opportunity. There's been many of us who've HAD the opportunity who blow it.

—Marjorie, an African American woman in her 30s

The *Blocked Opportunities* perspective on crime has its social scientific roots in Robert K. Merton's 1938 essay "Social Structure and Anomie." Crime, Merton held, results from a disjuncture between socially prescribed goals and the institutionally available means for goal attainment. American culture, on the one hand, inculcates a desire for material success—for the "American Dream"—while American economic arrangements, on the other, render attainment of material success by legitimate means impossible for many. This contradiction between goals and means exerts pressure on individuals. To reduce this pressure, individuals adopt one of five possible "modes of adaptation." Two of these involve at least some behaviors which are conventionally regarded as criminal. It is with these that we will be concerned.

One mode of adaptation available to individuals who discover their means to material success blocked is *innovation*. This involves resorting to illegitimate means—typically crime—to achieve conventional goals. In effect, the innovator sacrifices her commitment to institutionally sanctioned behavior in order to satisfy her enduring attachment to the culturally prescribed goal of material success. For Merton, the archetypal innovator was Al Capone, a figure who "represents the triumph of amoral intelligence over morally prescribed 'failure'" (1938:679).

The second mode of adaptation is *retreatism*. The retreatist is one who abandons both socially prescribed goals *and* institutionally sanctioned behavior; unable to achieve material success by legitimate means, but unwilling or unable to innovate, she adapts to the unbearable situation by escaping society altogether. For Merton, typical retreatists include "[p]sychotics, psychoneurotics, chronic autists, pariahs, outcasts, vagrants, vagabonds, tramps, chronic drunkards and drug addicts" (1938: 677).

Merton's theory is of such enduring importance because it specifies several concrete ways in which relative deprivation gets translated into criminal acts. In this chapter, in examining contemporary discourse on crime, we will encounter ideational material that is, at least in part, a popular sedimentation of Merton's formal theoretical writing.

BLOCKED OPPORTUNITIES IN THE OP EDS

Figure 5.1 compares *Blocked Opportunities'* performance in the op ed sample with those of *Faulty System* and *Social Breakdown*. As we can see, the frame appeared in a supportive light in 33% of the op eds (a bit less frequently than *Social Breakdown*) and was conjured in 10% for the purpose of rebuttal. Its overall performance was thus the weakest of the three frameworks.

Blocked Opportunities frequently appeared in the discourse as a counterpoint to *Faulty System:* of the 19 items that featured positive displays of the former, 11 also featured rebuttals of the latter. The relationship appears even stronger in the reverse: of the six items that featured

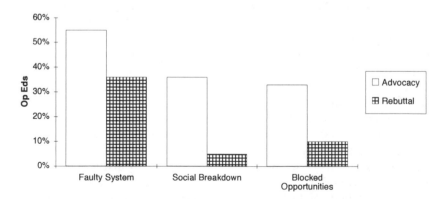

Figure 5.1.   Faulty System, Social Breakdown and Blocked Opportunities
        in the op eds.

rebuttals of *Blocked Opportunities,* five also featured positive displays of *Faulty System.* By way of illustration, the following excerpt from a Tom Wicker column in the *New York Times* begins with a rebuttal of *Faulty System,* and then promotes *Blocked Opportunities* by expressing some of its key prognostic elements:

> In the U.S., in the last two decades, the death penalty has been reinstated (in any state that opts for it), the prison population has been doubled, sentences generally are longer and less flexible, parole in some jurisdictions has been eliminated, peacekeeping forces have been increased. . . . Crime, however, has steadily increased, not just in New York but across the nation. . . . More jobs, better housing, decent medical care, improved education, greater opportunity—in the long run, all might be more useful than more police. (Wicker, 1990)

The frame was keyed through its diagnostic dimension in 10 op eds (17%). One such item merely mentioned education, poverty and housing among a series of crime-causing factors. The others, however, offered—at least implicitly—a more concrete image of the mechanism by which poverty or relative deprivation gets translated into street crime. A basic distinction can be drawn here between pieces that constructed the offender as one of Merton's innovators and pieces that constructed him or her as one of Merton's retreatists. In drawing this distinction in contemporary discourse the crucial issue is whether the offender is constructed as a rational actor in pursuit of material success (the innovator), or as an arational actor whose behavior is essentially expressive (the retreatist).

Seven columns fit into the former category. These items attributed crime to "hopelessness," "despair," "not enough jobs" and "nothing to lose." They share in common a depiction of the offender as one who would like to succeed by legitimate means but finds his or her way blocked. Frustrated, the would-be conformist turns to crime. The following claim in a *New York Times* op-ed by Michael Z. Letwin is typical:

> The immense artificially inflated profit in illegal drugs combined with dwindling economic opportunity, draws young people into the low level trade. (Letwin, 1990)

Three op eds expressed the retreatist imagery. These had in common attributions for street crime to "anger," "hate," and "rage." Here inequality was depicted as a source for emotions that generate violence. The following example is from a *New York Times* column by psychology professor Kenneth B. Clark.

Our society does not ask itself, "How do so many young people become mindlessly antisocial and, at times, self-destructive?" A painfully disturbing answer to this core question is that "mugged communities," "mugged neighborhoods" and, probably most importantly, "mugged schools" spawn urban "muggers." Given this fact, a more severe criminal justice system, more prisons and more citizen shootings will not solve the problem of urban crime. These are selective forms of anger directed toward the visible "muggers." The educationally rejected and despised "muggers"—the pool of unemployed and unemployable from which they come—will increase in numbers, defiance and venom. Not able to express their frustrations in words, their indignation takes the form of more crime. (Clark, 1990)

The frame was keyed through its prognostic dimension in 11 op eds (19%). These columns generally called for more social programs aimed at creating opportunities for inner-city residents. The last sentence in the excerpt from the Wicker column (above) is typical of these passages. Between "jobs, housing, medical care and education," jobs and job training are the most important in this sample; seven of the eleven items that featured a display of the frame's prognostic dimension called for either more jobs or more job training.

Finally, six items in the op ed sample (10%) conjured the frame for the purpose of rebuttal. Among these, two types can be discerned. The first includes rejections of the "liberal" approach to crime control, as in "The liberal solutions to our crime problems simply won't work" (Neely, 1990). The second includes items that charge that liberal rhetoric about crime, because it "excuses" criminal behavior, is in fact a source of the problem. Consider the following illustration from a *Chicago Tribune* op ed by Patrick T. Murphy:

The '60s ushered in the view that because the poor and the disadvantaged are victims, they should not be held fully responsible for their actions. The thug who knocks down the old lady and steals her purse is a victim of poverty. . . . Parents who pour scalding water on their children as punishment get their kids back because after all, they are poor and frustrated. The message is simple: You are not responsible for your actions. . . . The view that the poor are victims and so have diminished responsibility for their actions is paternalistic. Over the past 25 years it has caused increased misery and poverty among the very people it attempts to help. And it has caused untold horrors for the rest of us. (Murphy, 1990)

As we shall see, this last line of argument was echoed in many of the peer group discussions.

BLOCKED OPPORTUNITIES IN THE DISCUSSIONS

Assessing the performance of *Blocked Opportunities* in the discussions requires that we refine our measurement technique. In five discussions participants barely touched on the frame; they did not key it spontaneously, and in response to the facilitator's trigger statement they either muttered a few words indicating agreement or dissent, and then fell silent, or they changed the subject altogether (see, for example, Sandy's response to the *Blocked Opportunities* trigger statement in Chapter 4, p. 75). Transcripts of these discussions averaged 20 single-spaced pages in length, but each included less than one-half page of discourse relevant to *Blocked Opportunities*. We shall regard the frame's performance in these discussions as "weak."

Figure 5.2 compares the performances of *Blocked Opportunities, Social Breakdown* and *Faulty System*. We can see immediately that the overall showing of *Blocked Opportunities* was far and away the weakest of the three frames: It was strong in just 15% of the discussions and weak in a striking 40%. In the remaining 45% of the discussions the frame's ideational contents were contested. But this aggregate figure obscures a qualitative difference between disagreements over *Blocked Opportunities* and disagreements over the other frames: Whereas participants who contested either *Faulty System* or *Social Breakdown* tended to challenge one or another aspect of the frame, participants who contested *Blocked Opportunities* tended to reject it altogether. Moreover, while opponents of *Social Breakdown* and *Faulty System* were typically minority voices in their

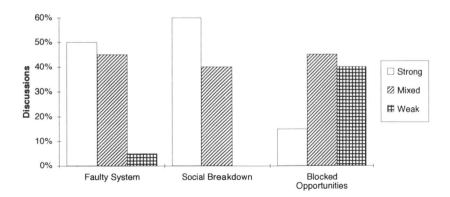

Figure 5.2. Faulty System, Social Breakdown and Blocked Opportunities in the discussions.

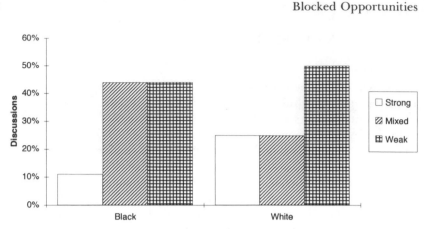

Figure 5.3.   Blocked Opportunities in the discussions, by race.

groups, opponents of *Blocked Opportunities* were almost always majorities. These distinctions will become clear in the discussion below.

As Figure 5.3 indicates, racial differences with respect to the overall performance of *Blocked Opportunities* were insignificant.

SUPPORTIVE ARGUMENTS

How did the discussion participants conjure *Blocked Opportunities?* How does their discourse compare with the discourse of the op ed writers? In the sections that follow, we will consider three lines of argument: The first and second conjure the frame through its diagnostic and prognostic dimensions, respectively; the third conjures the frame through discourse on an alleged disjuncture between culturally prescribed goals and institutionally available means for goal attainment.

Criminals as Innovators and Retreatists

In the peer group discussions, as in the public discourse, we can discern contrasting constructions of offenders as both innovators and retreatists. Both types of construction typically appear in brief passages consisting of a sentence or two. The innovator imagery, however, is more common, appearing in 50% of the discussions in comparison with 25% for the retreatist imagery. The following example of innovator imagery comes from the discussion of a black group. In it we hear the participants arguing about the relationship between poverty and crime. They are responding to the statement used to trigger the frame (Appendix A, question 3, statement 2). In the final utterance, Sarah presents a clear display of innovator imagery:

Group: Main Street:
Cast: (See p. 66)

Ben: Jobless, starvation, poverty goes on, yet I think that question is asking us if we think it's an excuse . . .

Helen: Not really.

Ben: Excuse or a reason.

Helen: Some people will find an excuse. But really if most of those things were addressed—I think—That's the way out. That's the way out.

Gloria: People will change.

Sarah: People would take a loaf of bread to feed their kids if they don't have it. It's hard for parents to see their children hungry. And it happens.

"People would take a loaf of bread to feed their kids," Sarah insists. Crime, in other words, is sometimes born of necessity.

In a second example, this time from a group of white professionals, we see a version of the argument that closely resembles the public discourse. These speakers are also responding to the statement used to trigger the frame.

Group: Holyoke Street
Cast:

Carol, a housing planner with more than a college degree, white, in her late 30s.
Janet, a marketing director and college graduate, white, in her mid 30s.
Ellen, a graduate student, white, in her late 20s.

Facilitator: O.K. Second statement. "Crime stems from poverty, unemployment, poor education, bad housing . . . [reads rest of statement]"

Carol: I strongly agree. I don't think it's just disadvantaged kids, but I think a lot of kids right now don't see a lot of options to minimum wage jobs, because all they are offering people in this country are service jobs which don't have any ability to progress or to be promoted, and all of our manufacturing jobs that go on to Third

World countries. And there's just not a lot of upward
mobility for people and who want to work at minimum
wage.

Ellen: You can't survive on that.

Carol: Right.

Janet: But I think it's hard in our society. It's hard to grow up
in this culture that says you're not something unless
you have something.

The transition from a manufacturing to a service-based economy, Carol
argues, has restricted job opportunities for young people to those that
pay the minimum wage. This state of affairs precipitates crime, her
fellow group members conclude, because "You can't survive on that,"
and because "It's hard to grow up in this culture that says you're not
something unless you have something."

In one final example, Charles, the African American mental health
worker introduced in Chapter 4 (see p. 74), draws upon his personal
experience to make a point about the relationship between work and
crime. He is responding to the claim, advanced a few moments earlier by
a fellow member of his group and appearing in the epigram to this
chapter, that opportunities for African Americans are plentiful.

Group: Longwood Road

Charles: It's family values, you know. I was fortunate enough to,
you know, we were poor and didn't have this, and had to
go without this, and had to walk to school five miles and
pack your own lunch, and all that stuff. But the thing
about it was, like Alice and her family, you know, I had a
mother and father who was there to guide me through.
They said "You want money? Go work for it!" I was fortunate enough to be, you know, in that era where there
were jobs—to me were plentiful. Because at least I always
went out and I looked and I asked. And you know I did a
little research, and I always was—Today it's a whole different ball game. There's no work out there for nobody.
They're laying off. They're cutting this, they're cutting
that. The financing is this. The budget is gone. We don't
have this. And then, like Marjorie is saying, I can't agree
with that now, especially for maybe young black people
today who are coming up, who don't have the same opportunities I've had. When I was coming up, their age, I
mean I could just go down the street and get a job in O.J.'s

car wash, or Rothstein's flower distributors. And it wasn't a great job or career, but I could always make some money. I didn't have to turn to crime to feed myself or to feed my family or anything like that.

Charles feels himself fortunate. Not only did he have supportive parents, he also came of age at a time when jobs were plentiful. In contrast to young people today, Charles is saying, he "didn't have to turn to crime" to feed himself or to feed his family.

Discourse that constructs offenders as retreatists tended to occur in the context of discussions of either drug abuse, domestic violence, or violence among young black men. Jane's depiction of the typical drug offender in the excerpt that follows is a good example. The conversationalists, all white, are responding to question 2: "Experts disagree about whether the crime problem is getting worse or better. In your opinion, is the crime problem getting worse or better, and why?"

Group: Dean Avenue
Cast: (See p. 49)
New Additions:

Eleanor, a vice president in charge of marketing and college graduate, in her late 30s.
Jane, a librarian with more than a college degree, in her mid 40s.
Carolyn, an engineering technician and college graduate, in her mid 40s.

    Bill: It's getting worse and it's going to get worse until they can fight the war on drugs. I think that's the whole basic [problem] behind everything. Every street corner you walk, you see them, you know?

Eleanor: Do you really think that we as a nation will ever get anywhere close to solving this drug problem?

    Bill: I hope so.

Susan: Until our values turn around, I don't think so.

              [unintelligible comment]

Carolyn: Money talks like he said.

Eleanor: If people don't have respect for themselves and their own bodies, so they're not going to respect others.

    Jane: Yeah but as the economy turns around and these people feel more secure economically, people of our kind are not going to need to hide in drugs or in alcohol, or you know, whatever.

> *Eleanor:*   Yeah, that's probably true.
>   *Jane:*   They're going to feel secure they've got a job, they're not
>   afraid of losing it, so that will cut back on it because the
>   market will decrease to some extent just because the
>   economy is better.
> *Eleanor:*   Yeah, I think the economy has a lot to do with it.

In Jane's discourse, people of the type in her discussion group use drugs when they feel insecure. A stronger economy will provide more jobs, diminish feelings of insecurity, and hence undermine the market for illicit drugs. The same kind of reasoning could be heard in several groups in connection with discourse on domestic violence and violence among young black men.

Good Jobs, Big Money

In most instances, calls for jobs, job training and education initiatives, for the purpose of reducing crime, were coded as expressions of *Blocked Opportunities*. The exceptional cases, coded as instances of *Social Breakdown,* were the occasional calls for job and education initiatives explicitly for the purpose of enhancing informal social control (see p. 75).

Calls for jobs, job training, education and housing initiatives, for the purpose of expanding opportunities and thereby reducing crime, could be heard in 70% of the discussions. Racial differences were insignificant; these arguments were expressed in 78% of the black and 63% of the white groups. The following illustration, taken from the speech of an African American woman in her late 40s, is more or less typical:

Group: Concord Street

> *Harriet:*   I really think we need to help the young people get a *good*
>   job, because what they're really looking for is money. Not a
>   little bit of money. They want money. That's just what this
>   selling does. They want *big* money. And they don't have the
>   education to get it. They need to educate the kids from the
>   beginning, let them know—Start educating them from
>   small, and keep on educating them. And give them some
>   big money, I guess. Because that's what they seem to want.

The way to stop young people from selling drugs, Harriet is saying, is to help them get jobs. But not any job will do; if we really want to stop crime, we must prepare children for *good* jobs that pay *big* money, because "that's what they seem to want."

The Other World Out There

The third argument closely mirrors the basic "anomie" theory advanced by Merton and described in the first part of this chapter. Recall that in its simplest form, the theory holds that crime stems from a disjuncture between culturally prescribed goals and institutionally available means for goal attainment. It was articulated by discussion participants in two black and three white groups. In the excerpt that follows, Henry, the African American police officer quoted in the two previous chapters, explains the roots of crime in a fashion that improves upon Merton's formulation in its persuasiveness. Henry is responding to a member of his group who a few moments earlier advocated youth activities for the purpose of crime reduction.

Group: Grove Hills Parkway

Henry: Activities are fine and dandy. They last so long, a couple hours or whatever, and then the kid gotta go home. Y'know, nasty, stinkin' house. Ain't nothing to eat. Dismal, y'know? A parent that, you know, is suffering. And looks at this TV, and the show is this other world out there where everything is bright and shining and ["hoyty toyty" —a voice interjects]. People have the gall to think that this phony activity they set up over here is gonna mollify or, you know, tone that down? That kid has desires. And they see them in the middle of a dump, a trash situation. What kind of hope is he gonna, you know—Do you think that activities for this kind of kid is gonna pump him up? Ahhh.

In a similar vein, an African American woman in a black group argued that sports celebrities Michael Jordan and Magic Johnson, because they appear in advertisements for high-priced sneakers, are in part responsible for the crime problem. The advertisements, the woman contended, are targeted at inner-city kids who could not possibly afford the footwear. "How would you market something like that when you're trying to help your people? You know one thing my mother always said, never forget where *you* came from!"

REBUTTAL ARGUMENTS

Blocked Opportunities was rebutted more frequently and with greater zeal than either *Faulty System* or *Social Breakdown*. In this section, we will consider four lines of argument advanced *against* the frame.

Poverty Does NOT Cause Crime

The most important rebuttal argument, expressed in 13 discussions (65%), holds simply that poverty is *not* a cause of crime. There are three versions of this argument, each important to the participants' regard for the frame.

Version I

The first version claims that since most poor people do not turn to crime, poverty, per se, cannot be considered one of crime's causes. The following illustration is excerpted from the discussion of a black group. The speaker is an unemployed African American woman in her late 20s.

Group: Concord Street

June: I think that it's been more of a stereotype to say that poverty, discrimination and different things—You know, like you said, those are factors that could come into play. But I think, like she said, because a person is poor doesn't mean that they're gonna go out and do all these things. There are poor people that you know are very—They're not criminals. They live their life just as normal as everybody else and I think that—like she said, the media has really stereotyped, especially like single parents and different things of all this nature. There are a lot of people that grew up in single-parent families that are fine. They're not criminals. Their mother or their father really brought them up in a good way.

To suggest that poverty causes crime, June is saying, is to stereotype the poor. In reality, poor people "live their life just as normal as everybody else."

Another example of the same kind of argumentation comes from a white group. In the following excerpt, Alex, the television producer quoted in the introduction and in Chapter 3, evokes the historical example (mentioned in another white group as well) of European immigrants who "pulled themselves up."

Group: Jacob's Lane
Cast: (See p. 78)

Alex: It's hard to give these kids a desire. And that's what to me it boils down to, is giving them the desire to be better. I don't mean not crime-ridden, but again if we're looking at history—and that's what this is that we're living now—will

soon be history in some years. What about the people
who—and granted they may have been Caucasian—but
what about the people who came here from Italy, Europe,
Germany, Russia . . .

Paula: There's always been crime in poor neighborhoods.

Alex: I agree. But what happened is they would start working
hard to pull themselves up. Does that stop because now
suddenly you're Black or Puerto Rican or Hispanic? No!

Paula: I just think they have additional challenges.

That European immigrants were able to work their way out of poverty,
Alex is arguing, is evidence that no inexorable relationship exists between
impecuniousness and crime. The key, Alex insists, is cultivating among
youthful members of contemporary minority groups "the desire."

Version II

The second version of the argument insists that attributing crime to
poverty is merely "making excuses." Race differences are conspicuous
here; this version was advanced in five black but just one white group. In
the example that follows, an African American woman in her early 40s
concludes a personal experience narrative about overcoming poverty
with the moral "You can make it." Attributing crime to poverty, she
insists, is strictly for "weak minded people." The speaker is a high school
graduate and works as an "order picker." She is responding to the statement used to trigger the frame.

Group: Woodman Road

Clara: All right. And I'm going to tell you why I disagree on that.
There were seven of us, O.K.?, in my family. A lot of
days—nights, my mother went to bed hungry to feed us.
We may not have had meat on the table. But we had something on that table. I didn't know what a lot of things were
until I was fourteen years old—old enough to go to work
for myself after school. I worked every two weeks, and
made $32.80 every two weeks. I would go home and give
my mother $10.00 to buy milk and bread. The rest I would
save to buy me a leather coat, sneakers, the things I needed.
So it's not poverty. If you want to make something of yourself, you can. You might have a struggle. But you can make
it. So I don't agree with this poverty and all this other stuff
that they're talking about. Those are for weak-minded
people.

Version III

Clara's speech also contains an example of the third version of the argument. In nine discussions—four black, two white and three mixed—speakers told personal experience narratives about growing up poor. These narratives were shared to make the point that poverty does not inexorably lead to crime. The stories were often quite detailed and clearly important to their tellers. In the interests of economy, we will restrict our consideration to just one more. The following example is from another black group. The speaker is Alice, an African American woman whom we first met in Chapter 3 (see p. 52). She is responding to the statement used to trigger the frame, which read in part "Crime stems from poverty, unemployment, poor education, bad housing, inadequate health care and discrimination. . . ."

Group: Longwood Road

Alice: I think—I grew up with all these—all those things you say, but it didn't make me go out there. My parents were the structure that Charles is talking about. My parents were there. We were poor. There were 11 of us. I mean we had all those things and—no, I don't think—It doesn't make you grow up feeling a great deal proud of who you are as a black person, but at the same time, I think the support and love I got from my parents encouraged me to grow up to be who I am and be a responsible adult. I have six brothers and they're not out there trying to be in the wild wild west. Both of them—the younger two—are born-again Christians. So I don't think that all that causes people to turn to crime. I think it's people's perspectives on life and what foundation they're brought up on. We were also brought up in church until we were 18, and then we were given a choice that we could decide whether we were going to continue or not. So we were poor and did all those things and very happy, so, you know—that's one side of it. I'm sure there are other people that don't have that family support and then turn to crime I guess. I mean, I don't know.

Alice grew up poor but neither she nor her six brothers behave as if "trying to be in the wild wild West." The key to their success, Alice believes, is the "support and love" they received from their parents. The lesson Alice is drawing is clear: loving families, not material comforts, are the key to discouraging crime.

It's a Personal Choice

The second rebuttal argument, expressed in three black, four white and one mixed group, holds that offenders *choose* crime because it is either easier or more lucrative than legitimate employment. In five groups this argument was expressed specifically in reference to the drug trade. The following example comes from the discussion of a white group. Note that the excerpt also contains yet another example of the personal experience narrative described above. Christine, an administrative assistant in her early 20s, is responding to the statement used to trigger the frame.

Group: Gordon Road
Cast: (See p. 38)

Christine: I strongly disagree. I'm an inner city kid. I went to school. I made the choice to get an education, and even though I went to school with some animals, I got an education. I went on an interview, I spoke properly, I got a job, and I started working when I was 15. And most of my friends did the same. The kids that were lazy and didn't want to do it, didn't. And *that's* why they turned to crime, because they were too lazy and didn't want to have to work. They wanted to be able to say, oh, I'm going to work from ten to midnight tonight, and I'm going to sell these drugs, and I'm going to make this much money that you're not going to make in a month.

Martha: They wanted instant success without working for it.

Christine: It's a personal choice. It doesn't matter where you live or what school you go to. You can get an education at any school you're in. It's just a choice you make whether you do it or you don't. From an inner-city kid.

Although she went to school with some animals, Christine made the decision to get an education, to go on an interview, and at the interview to speak properly. Her classmates who became drug dealers were simply lazy; they preferred making quick money to exerting effort at a legitimate job.

It's Not Just the Poor

The third rebuttal argument attacks the frame's tacit claim that crime is principally the work of poor people. In four of the six groups in which this argument was expressed, speakers referred to the frame's inability to make sense of white collar crime, in particular the Savings and Loan debacle. In the following excerpt, from a black group, the speakers are especially impressed with the exploits of junk-bond trader Michael Milken.

Group: Peach Tree Lane
Cast: (See p. 40)
New Additions:

Louise, a nurse clinician with more than a college degree, African American, in her early 60s.
Ertha, a homemaker who did not finish high school, African American, in her early 70s.

Louise:	I don't fully agree with that, because all the crimes are not committed by poor people or ignorant people. There's much white collar crime.
Margaret:	Now it's a funny kind of crime like that Milliken. Now they just reduced his sentence to two years. You know that man made billions?
William:	Yeah, white collar crime.
Margaret:	When he comes out he has a billion dollars.
Unknown voice:	A brilliant mind.
Unknown voice:	Is that horrible?!
William:	People see that, then keep going, because if he can do that, then ["They can do it"—voices interject]. I could spend a few years—Hey, I'm a pretty honest guy, but if I can make a few million dollars, go to jail for three, four years, even five, I'll do it! [laughter and clamor] As long as I don't kill anybody.
Ertha:	I'll go a year. I'm not going three or four years. [clamor for a few seconds, laughter] One year I'll go to jail for. I'll be with you for one year.

Opportunities Abound

The final rebuttal argument, expressed in two black and two white groups, asserts that opportunities for poor people or people of color are in fact plentiful. An example of this argument appears as Marjorie's contribution to the epigram for this chapter. An additional example, this one with a notably harsher edge to it, comes from the discussion of a working class white group. Phyllis is responding to the statement used to trigger the frame:

Group: Hallibut Square
Cast: (See p. 46)

Phyllis: I think everybody around here, I don't know, I think the kids—[over interruptions] I think what this is saying too is like these down in the project where I helped—you know, the poor, disadvantaged [edge of sarcasm in the speaker's voice]. They're no more disadvantaged than I am! They all went to school with my kids. Right? They probably have more money than I had.

Bob: We were brought up to like respect other people's property, and stuff like that. You don't see that anymore.

Janet: Sometimes I think that they're given too much, and they expect. They expect. Where we had to go out at 15 years of age and get a job. If you wanted a skirt for a dance, you went out and got a job and you bought your own.

[A few paragraphs further down in the transcript:]

Phyllis: [Reading from the facilitator's question sheet:] "Inner-city kids turn to crime because they don't see any opportunities for legitimate work." The kids in the suburbs don't have any more opportunities than the kids in the inner city do.

Janet: Actually, kids in the inner city, there's more jobs for them than there are in the suburbs.

Bob: Than there is out in the suburbs. Exactly.

Janet: That's a lot of hogwash [referring to the trigger statement].

Phyllis: We're crossing that statement right out of here.

[laughter]

"There's more jobs for them than there are in the suburbs," Janet insist. How then can anyone attribute crime to "blocked opportunities"?

CONCLUSION

Blocked Opportunities was displayed in a positive fashion in fewer than one-third of the op eds. Contrary to the claims of some analysts (e.g., Elias 1993:6–25), the frame is clearly "available" in the public discourse on crime. But it is just as clearly subordinate to *Faulty System* and *Social Breakdown* in the ongoing symbolic contest.

Turning to the discussions, the frame's performance was weak in 40% and strong in just 15%. In the nine groups in which the frame was contested, voices raised against it were the most fervid: they spoke for longer; they spoke with greater intensity; and they drew more heavily on personal experiences. These findings, like those presented in Chapter 3, lend support to the conventional wisdom on public opinion about crime: Much as people tended to embrace the law and order frame *Faulty System*, they tended to reject its liberal rival *Blocked Opportunities*.

Why did *Blocked Opportunities* perform so poorly in the discussions? Why did *Faulty System* and *Social Breakdown* perform so well? What can these findings tell us about the political and public policy significance of our society's preoccupation with crime? We will address these questions shortly. First we must examine the performances of the remaining frames *Media Violence* and *Racist System*.

6

MEDIA VIOLENCE AND
RACIST SYSTEM

A complete account of the conversationalists' discourse on crime requires that we consider two additional frameworks: *Racist System* and
Media Violence. These two are treated as *secondary frames* because discourse displaying their key elements was much less prominent in the op
eds and discussions than discourse displaying *Blocked Opportunities, Social
Breakdown* or *Faulty System*. "Secondary framework" is thus a designation
based upon an empirical observation rather than a normative judgment
or deductive inference.

I should note, however, that *Racist System* and *Media Violence* were
introduced into the discussions in ways distinct from the other frames.
In Chapter 2, I explained the rationale behind the decision to trigger
Racist System with a question about a highly publicized murder investigation. As I will show, my initial feeling that the sensitive nature
of talk about race and crime demanded such an *indirect* approach was
amply borne out. The possibility exists, in any case, that the relative
paucity of discourse displaying *Racist System* is related to the study
design.

Media Violence is a different matter altogether. Where this frame entered the discussions, it did so spontaneously. The interview schedule
did not attempt in any way to trigger the frame. In fact, I decided to
consider the relevant discourse only after examining the transcripts.

Both frames can be traced backward in criminological theory, but
their ancestry is more diverse than in the cases considered thus far.
Media Violence is rooted in notions concerning imitation that extend
backward to the work of the nineteenth century French scholar Gabriel
Tarde (Beirne, 1993). Adumbrations of the frame can also be found in
the writings of American criminologist Edwin Sutherland (1955). In
promoting his theory of "differential association," Sutherland argued
that the propensity for crime is learned from parents, peers, teachers,
and other close associates. While the role of the primary group was
clearly most important to the theory, the eminent criminologist also con-

sidered the mass media to be a potentially important agent of socialization into conformist and criminal values.

Racist System has criminological roots in both labeling and conflict theory. To the extent that the frame offers an attribution for crime, it is one informed by the former. Labeling theorists (Lemert, 1972; Becker, 1963) insist that criminal careers (what they call "secondary deviance") are the result of the successful labeling of particular youthful offenders as delinquents. Once successfully attached to an individual, the "delinquent" label influences both the individual's self-concept and how others behave toward him or her. By these means the label creates a "self-fulfilling prophecy," impelling, for example, a youth guilty of only innocent hijinks into commission of more serious and more frequent crimes. *Racist System* borrows this line of argument when it suggests that police harassment of minority group members—or society's general expectations concerning their alleged criminal propensities—are actual *causes* of crime.

The frame's floodlight is not generally cast on the causes of crime, however, but on police, judicial and political reaction to it. In this regard it echoes the views of conflict theorists such as Richard Quinney (1970, 1974). The Marxist criminologist argued that the state's agencies of social control can best be understood as tools in the class struggle. If (as Quinney believes) the criminal acts of the poor are policed and punished vigorously while the criminal acts of the rich are for the most part ignored, it is because the criminal justice system plays a key role in reinforcing, through ideology and brute force, an unjust capitalist social order. The conversationalists key a variation on this theme when they insist that the white power structure either generates or tolerates inner-city drug trafficking in order to eliminate, through street violence or police crackdown, a stratum of jobless, angry and potentially rebellious young black men.

We take up the secondary frameworks in turn, beginning with *Media Violence*. First we consider its performance in the op ed sample.

MEDIA VIOLENCE IN THE OP EDS

Figure 6.1 compares *Media Violence's* performance with those of the other frames. As we can see, the frame was conjured in a positive fashion in just 5% of the op eds. All frame displays were in the *Washington Post,* two in op eds by columnist George Will and one in a piece by psychiatrist Charles Krauthammer. No need to construct an elaborate typology here as all three pieces presented the same basic claim: Depictions of killings and mayhem in the mass media *glorify* violence and *cheapen* regard for

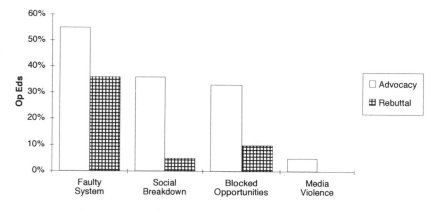

Figure 6.1. Media Violence and other frames in the op eds.

life. I will quote Krauthammer's piece at length as it is a paradigmatic expression of the frame:

> [T]hat American popular culture is drenched in sex and violence and a degrading combination of the two is a truism. But it is then hard to understand the surprise that greets the resulting degradation and depravity of real life: a quadrupling of rapes in 30 years, random shootings of children . . . a doubling of the number of youths shot to death in the last six years alone. . . . Kids see 10,000 killings on TV by age 18. Is it any wonder that a growing number might like to commit just one? Sexual aggression and misogyny are celebrated in rap. Is it any wonder that kids arrested for rape and murder are utterly conscienceless and uncomprehending? . . . As a psychiatrist, I used to see psychotic patients who, urged on by voices inside their heads, did crazy and terrible things, like immolating themselves. Now we have legions of kids walking around with the technological equivalent: 2 Live Crew wired by Walkman directly into their brains, proposing to "bust you [. . . expletive] then break your backbone . . . I wanna see you bleed." Surprised that a whole generation is busting and breaking and bleeding? Culture has consequences. (Krauthammer, 1990)

The op ed sample included no rebuttals of *Media Violence.* Apparently, in the elite public discourse, the notion that "culture has consequences" is undisputed.

MEDIA VIOLENCE IN THE DISCUSSIONS

Because the secondary frames were introduced in the discussions in unique ways, we must assess their performances in their own terms rather than in comparison with the other frameworks. *Media Violence* could be heard in five discussions, always in a positive fashion. Race differences were not striking: the frame was expressed in three white, one black and one mixed group (in the latter by an African American participant). The central message of these displays was identical to that of the public discourse: The mass media glorifies violence, cultivating in young viewers an urge for imitation. Consider the following example in which Alex, the TV producer introduced in previous chapters (he is also a former radio talk-show host), asserts that when it comes to TV violence, the "medium is the message."

Group: Jacob's Lane
(See p. 1)

[In response to the question: What crimes are you most concerned about and who is doing these crimes?]

Geraldine: I fear the violence of television. I really do. You know when I'm watching it and I'm thinking about a show like this—one program coming on tomorrow night— prime time, like five o'clock. How many children really would be watching? And I honestly say boys and girls at the age of like 13 or 14 are imitating what they see in violence. And I think it really is [up to us] as a group to try to do something to clean up television.

[Further down in the transcript:]

Alex: And I go again with what Geraldine said—and I've said this too when I'm doing a radio show—you look at the movies that are popular and kids see the most violent person in the movie is the most successful—Rambo, the

Terminator, whatever it is. So the more firepower you have—the more knives, guns—the more you can beat somebody up or cut them up—you end up as a winner. And they see that, and they think, well, and if I carry a gun and I shoot another kid, well then I'll be the winner because he'll be gone.

Carol: And I think some of the new films that are coming out— the *New Jack City, Boyz in the Hood*—

Alex: Juice.

Carol: Juice. Well, the overlying message is not what's happening. I mean they're usually saying, you know, don't do the drugs, don't hang out with the gangs and so forth. That's not what kids are identifying with. And—

Alex: The medium is the message is what it boils down to. If

they see the violence and they miss the message of don't
do it—all they see is the violence on the screen.

Some participants also struck the theme that young viewers of media
violence fail to distinguish between fantasy and reality, or, what is essentially the same thing, to grasp the finality and seriousness of death.
Consider this example:

Group: Peach Tree Lane
Cast: (See p. 102)
New Addition:

Rose: a homemaker and high school graduate, in her late 60s.

> *Ertha:* [The killings are] drug related but I don't think these
> kids have to be on drugs in order to kill. Seems like
> they're doing it on their own.
>
> *Rose:* There's so much TV.
>
> *Unknown:* They can't separate reality.
>
> *Ertha:* Just an argument will bring out a gun. Or they leave a
> hall or something, they come back with a gun.
>
> [Further down in the transcript:]
>
> *Margaret:* But it's sort of like a fantasy out there. Instead of the
> real world, you know. And it's almost like they live in
> fantasies instead of living responsible, real lives. I have
> a feeling that it has more to do with the fact that all
> of the movies are fantasies, all the TV is fantasy, even
> the guns that you were talking about—the toy guns—
> they're fantasy!
>
> *Rose:* They could change that if they wanted to. Just like
> we have everything bad, they could put good on. But
> sometimes I think—I don't know—it's like Moses time.

To the extent that TV violence is a cause of violence in the society, the
social problem strikes these conversationalists as easily remedied. Violence on TV must simply be banned or severely restricted. All that is
needed is the political will to act, and thus, "it's like Moses time."

RACIST SYSTEM IN THE OP EDS

As Figure 6.2 indicates, *Racist System* was conjured for the purpose of
advocacy in 10% of the op eds and in 7% for the purpose of rebuttal.
Two types of advocacy displays were most important. In the first, writers

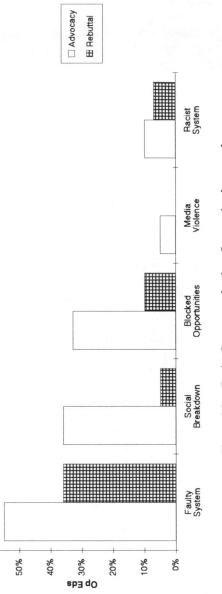

Figure 6.2. Racist System and other frames in the op eds.

decried the violation of Fourth Amendment rights of black men through police "brutality," "illegal searches and seizures" and "frame-ups." Twice such displays were triggered by the Los Angeles Police Department assault on motorist Rodney King. The example that follows is excerpted from a piece by *Chicago Tribune* columnist Clarence Page:

> Los Angeles Police Chief Daryl F. Gates wants you to believe his police have no prejudices. As W.C. Fields might say, they thrash everyone equally. That's just about how silly he sounded when he asserted that racial prejudice did not play a role in the infamous beating three of his department's white officers inflicted on Rodney G. King. . . . Whether it was sparked by racism or simple sadism, the shocking video . . . can only stir more antipathy toward police, particularly by poor blacks whose victimization by police may be outmatched only by their victimization by civilian criminals. (Page, 1991)

In the second type of advocacy display, writers allege a racial "double standard" in the administration of justice. This double standard is at least one reason blacks are arrested and imprisoned in numbers disproportionate to their share of the general population. Our example of this argument comes from a *New York Times* piece by Rutgers University professor Evan Stark:

> Blacks constitute 13 percent of the urban population, but, according to the Federal Bureau of Investigation, account for more than half of those arrested for murder, rape and nonnegligent manslaughter. This is five times the rate for whites. . . . The problem with using this information to draw conclusions is that its primary source—data on arrests and imprisonment—may itself by the product of racial discrimination. Our picture of black violence may be more a reflection of official attitudes and behavior than of racial differences. . . . The belief that blacks are "violence prone" leads to a double standard in police response. When white and black teen agers commit the same offense, police are seven times more likely to charge black teen agers with a felony, and courts are more likely to imprison the teen ager. (Stark, 1990)

More idiosyncratically, *Racist System* was conjured through the claim that police do not provide adequate protection to black communities; the claim that the stereotype of the young black offender encourages black youth to act out the role; and the claim that the death penalty is administered in a racist fashion.

Most of the rebuttal displays of the frame rejected the claim that police officers use excessive force in their dealings with criminal suspects. While none addressed the allegation that police brutality is motivated by racism, all were written in response to such claims. The rhetorical context for the op eds, therefore, rendered them unequivocal rejections of *Racist System*. The excerpt that illustrates this type of rebuttal comes from a *Los Angeles Times* op ed by patrol officer Susan Yocum:

> Regrettably, there may always be officers who react without restraint or compassion. But to accuse the department of maintaining brutality ignores the dangerous reality of our job. Often and increasingly, our actions are a necessary response to horrific situations. To confuse this with institutionalized brutality . . . is ridiculous. (Yocum, 1990)

Police behavior is governed by the nature of situations, Yocum is arguing, and not by the color of skin. To evoke W.C. Fields again—apologies to Clarence Page—the police thrash everyone equally.

RACIST SYSTEM IN THE DISCUSSIONS

The relationship between race, crime and criminal justice is for many a sensitive and emotionally charged topic. Fearing a breakdown of rapport between the facilitator and group members, I decided, perhaps naively, to trigger *Racist System* with a question about the so-called "Stuart affair." For the reader who missed the story's saturation media coverage (including the made-for-TV movie "A Murder in Boston"), the question referred to the 1989 murder of Carol Stuart apparently by her husband Charles. Carol Stuart was pregnant at the time of her murder; in fact, she was killed shortly after the couple drove away from the hospital where the two were attending a prenatal class. In the immediate aftermath of the incident, Charles Stuart, who was white, told police that his wife's assailant was a black man wearing a running suit. The police subsequently conducted an aggressive search of the largely black neighborhood adjacent to the hospital, sparking resident complaints of civil rights violations. The complaints reached a crescendo after Charles Stuart's brother, Matthew, tipped-off the state's attorney, and after Charles, with the police closing-in, committed suicide by jumping from a downtown bridge.

In the first five discussions the Stuart question was asked first, as a sort of topical "warm up" to the questions that would follow. But in two groups, one mixed and the other white, the question sparked immediate hostility. In the white group speakers complained that they were "bored" with the topic that had already received far too much media attention. In the mixed group, Al, a retired white cop, angrily complained that the question threatened the unity the group was working so hard to achieve:

Group: Park Terrace

Al: We were trying to get along in this neighborhood and now you
       bring up an issue like this and people are going to get on
       everybody's back. We're trying to get along. We're trying to
       live with each other. No problems. We're trying to let every-
       body do their own thing. And then you come along with a
       question like this and it's going to upset everything.

Recognizing the unexpectedly provocative nature of the question, I
decided to switch its place in the interview schedule. In the remaining
discussions the question was asked last on the theory that upon reaching
the final question the conversationalists would be more at ease with each
other and less wary of the facilitator. This strategy proved successful as
the question was willingly addressed by the remaining groups.[1]

That most of the discourse relevant to *Racist System* occurred following
the Stuart question raises a problem of interpretation. The Stuart case
has its own rich culture of competing interpretive frameworks. One
frame holds that the story is really about an abusive husband who finally
killed his pregnant wife. Another holds that the story is about a working
class kid who would do anything to achieve his "American dream." But
the frame that seems to have been nearly hegemonic in the media discourse highlights race: It holds that the story is about a white man who
played off popular racist assumptions about crime and criminals, and
about politicians, media personalities and police who were taken in by
the ploy. The dominant media interpretation of the facts surrounding
the murder of Carol Stuart, therefore, included key elements of *Racist
System*.

This state of affairs renders interpretation of the discussion transcripts a bit tricky: If the participants' discourse on the Boston murder
and its aftermath expresses elements of *Racist System,* we are left wonder-
ing whether that discourse is specific to the case at hand (i.e., a consequence of the media's preferred framing of the story) or reflective of a
more general orientation. In dealing with the actual transcripts, however, this problem did not prove insurmountable. It turns out to be
relatively easy to distinguish between claims concerning the Stuart case
in particular and claims concerning the operation of the criminal justice
system in general. In the account that follows, we shall consider both
types of claims, but we shall regard displays of *Racist System* in discourse
narrowly focused on the Stuart case as *weak displays* of the frame. Alter-
natively, we shall regard displays of the frame that make points about the
criminal justice system in general as *strong displays*.

Weak Displays

Conversationalists in four white, seven black and one mixed group charged that police or politicians responded to the murder of Carol Stuart in a racist or prejudiced fashion. In most cases they argued that police violated the civil rights of black men in the course of their search for the killer. Some criticized the treatment of Willie Bennett, the black man whom the police initially framed for the murder. As we might have expected, discourse of this sort was brief and vacillating in the white groups but fully developed and impassioned in the black ones. First consider examples from two white groups:

Group: Meadowbrook Street
Cast:

Sandy, a bank executive and college graduate, in her late 30s.
Jerry, a manager with a graduate degree, in his 50s.

Sandy: I think that after going through [the Stuart affair]—in terms of still today you're not quite sure in terms of whether it was handled improperly or properly. That it didn't do a very—it didn't do the Boston Police Department any credit in terms of how the whole thing was handled. Especially in terms of—you know—taking the quick identity and then going after every black male who had a black sweatshirt on and assuming that they were—

Unknown: The person.

Sandy: —the person, you know.

Jerry: It really left a bad taste in your mouth about some of the ethnic communities around here, too, how they are very bigoted.

Sandy is "not quite sure" whether the police reaction to the Stuart murder was appropriate. Similarly, in the excerpt that follows, another white participant "supposes" the police were "very rough" in conducting their search.

Group: Holyoke Street Group
Cast: (See p. 93)

Carol: I think [the Stuart affair] had a very devastating impact on the Mission Hill neighborhood. And I think it will take a long time for those people to trust the police again. Because I suppose the police were very rough, I mean they stopped any young black male—you know—everyone they saw was stopped and questioned and I think it will take a really long time for people to forget that.

One white participant seemed to be ready to generalize from the Stuart case to routine police practice but backed-off under challenge from others in his group:

Group: Jacob's Lane
Cast: (See p. 78)

Alex: Well, it makes you wonder, too, in that regard, that if he had said some white guy had come in and stolen his car, they would have been so quick to go find the white guy. Right away, because it was in Mission Hill, and he said it was black guy who shot them—whammo!— immediately they went and picked up the suspect because he was black. Literally. So I don't know, I just think that it was bad all around.

· Paula: (to Laura) What do you think?

Laura: I mean, I don't agree that just because he said it was a black man—I think that if he said a white person they would not have desire—They would have taken the same approach. They would have gone looking for a white man because—looking at Stuart himself first, because he was shot. I don't think it's *just* because he said he was black.

Alex: No, but I think that really carried a lot of weight with the police in that area. It just fell into place. There is a great deal of crime over there, and so naturally, assuming that the black man was named, it seemed to fall into place. I'm not [saying] they wouldn't have looked for a white man, but I wonder if they would have looked as hard.

Laura: But I think it's also an area where a lot of white people travel in that area—because of the hospital there are a lot of white people over there.

Carol: I think they would have looked as hard because of the nature of the crime.

Unknown: Yes.

Alex: Because she was pregnant.

Carol: Because she was pregnant, her baby was dead, and the whole business.

In this exchange, Alex begins by charging that the police response to Carol Stuart's murder was influenced by her husband's claim that the murderer was a black man. Had Charles Stuart claimed the murderer was white, Alex wonders, would the police have been as quick make an arrest even at the price of framing an innocent man? Laura rejects the insinuation of racist police behavior, countering that it was Charles Stuart's gunshot wound, and not his claims concerning the race of his alleged assailant, that made his version of events seem credible. Carol then jumps in, arguing that the police "looked so hard because of the nature of the crime." Faced with these challenges, Alex retreats, conceding in the end that the police department's zeal in pursuing Carol Stuart's murderer was related to the fact that she was pregnant at the time of her fatal assault (and hence, by implication, *unrelated* to Charles Stuart's claims concerning the race of the alleged assailant).

In contrast to the equivocal criticisms of the police voiced in the white groups, consider the following from a black group:

Group: Concord Street
Cast: (See p. 98)

(In response to the trigger question—see Appendix A, question 6:)

June: Boston is going to be known for [the Stuart case]. No one's gonna forget this—just like in L.A., Rodney King. . . . I think the Stuart case is not gonna be buried. It's gonna live on for a long time. It has a very negative effect because of the police and the police are brainwashed to a certain extent too—even by the media. This is why they tore these people's houses up and stuff. They're going in there busting people that don't got nothing to do with it. Butstin' down their house—you know what I'm saying? What is this?

June's discourse is not simply more vivid and impassioned than the discourse heard in the white groups. It also links the reaction of Boston police to the Stuart murder to the beating of Rodney King by Los Angeles police. In so doing, June is developing an argument about police behavior *in general*. This excerpt is thus also an example of a strong display of the frame.

Strong Displays

The move from specific to general expressions of *Racist System* could be heard in six black but in just one white group. In the latter, a speaker also mentioned the King episode, commenting that "there is a lot of brutality among law enforcement officers." But with that exception, *strong displays* of the frame were absent in the white discussions.

References to King comprised the largest category of strong displays in the black groups, appearing in five discussions including June's. But most speakers in these groups were more explicit than June in drawing out the message of the King beating. Consider the following from a speech by Martin, the firefighter introduced in Chapter 4.

Group: Longwood Road

Martin: Charles Stuart—Mission Hill Housing Projects—it's what goes on in every state of the nation. I mean it's nothing new. I see it happening with Charles Stuart, Rodney King, and I don't see it ever going to change. I mean we are a minority here and unless people learn to treat each other equally it's not going to change. I basically see it like that.

Charges of routine police harassment of blacks and other minorities *independent* of discourse on King could be heard in four black discussions. Recall for example Alice's insistence (Chapter 3, see p. 52) that increasing criminal justice punitiveness would mean that "all the black men in Boston are gonna be picked up, stripped, searched, and thrown in jail and doing time for a lot of things they haven't committed."

Participants also conjured the frame in four black groups by charging that the police and the courts use a "double standard" when it comes to blacks. This category of strong displays includes charges that minorities "do not get a fair shake within the criminal system," that whites receive preferential treatment, and that police are more likely to assume that a complaint is veridical when the alleged offender is black. The following excerpt contains instances of the latter two types of claim:

Group: Fisher Hill Road
Cast: (See p. 25)

Deborah: We see, you know, on national television, young black men just slammed up against walls and frisked down and all of that and you know just because they happened to be in a particular area at a particular hour. So—

Sam: The [Mafia] crime boss—who was that? Archa?

Deborah: Patriarcha.

Sam: Whatever. They had him—they had his handcuffs *in front* of him. Like to put his hands where he *want* to.

But [the hands of black suspects they put] in the back. So see, there's lots of differences in that, you know. No question about that.

Karl: It's racist. It's racism. In the State of Massachusetts— any way you look at it.

Unknown: No question, that's right.

Karl: And I don't know if you all know—Boston is the mother of this country and she's the mother of racism. She's the mother of this country and she's the mother of racism.

Sam: The only difference that makes it sound different here in Boston is—I was raised up in the South also—

Karl: Yeah, I was too.

Sam: —and here's the thing what happened: We know what's going on here. And these people here are racist. They know but they don't want to come out and admit it. That's the difference. See, they don't want to admit. They know they're racist but they'll come and smile in your face. And let them get behind your back—Don't you look at a girl! If you look at a girl and she happen to say rape—regardless, you are the one. Regardless, you're the one.

Racist System can also be conjured through the charge that courts and police do not provide "equal protection" to black neighborhoods. This argument was expressed in two black groups, including once by a speaker who stated that "a lot of us think that [if] we kill our people, nothing gonna be done, and usually it's not, and I think that's why they [keep] doing it."

Before turning to the frame rebuttals, there is one more type of *Racist System* display that warrants attention. In four black groups speakers argued that forces external to the black community are encouraging its destruction. The specific charge advanced in three of these groups is that inner-city drug trafficking is either tolerated or encouraged by the powers that be. Consider the following illustrations of this *conspiracy* argument:

Group: Peach Tree Lane
Cast: (See p. 102)

Margaret: Let me say a little something about that. I think that crime is introduced into our community. It's introduced by outside elements who find we are vulnerable. They come in with their drugs, they come in with their guns, they come in with the money and the incentives.

	And they find poor people, people that feel they're up against the wall, that don't have an education. You know. They're the people that they want to make their millions for them.
William:	You see them in flashy cars, good clothes.
Margaret:	Because where the poor people of these districts make hundreds, these people from outside make millions. . . . How many of us could bring in millions of dollars worth of marijuana? So they stick it to us. And just because we're vulnerable. We're at the bottom of the ladder, right? ["Right"—voices agree] And then they call us the criminals.
Unknown:	We're the victims!
Margaret:	Because they stand on the outside, you know, *clean.* They live in the suburbs and people don't even know. They say "We have lovely neighbors" you know? "They dress so nice, they have good cars, they have lovely homes." And they don't know that they are the ones that are feeding these districts.
Ertha:	That's why they can bring all the guns and things in.
Margaret:	Yeah, because they look so nice.
Ertha:	They got the boats to bring the stuff in and they own the little small planes which they just, whoosh, right over our heads.
Margaret:	There's a kind of genocide going on. I mean everything is slanted if you know what I mean. The idea is that we're the criminals, you know, and we can't be educated. There's a lot of slant going on. We have the most diseases. We die earlier. We're killing each other off, you know? Things like that. This keeps on going, and going, and going. And it's designed to make us the kind of people that nobody would have any pity for. See, so if they ruin Roxbury, there's nobody in those other districts that give a damn! Because they're the kind of people that have those diseases, least educated. Not just poverty, we're just no good!

Margaret seems to be arguing that the powerful tolerate drug pushing in inner city neighborhoods in order to foster a negative image of African Americans. Their goal, in Margaret's view, is to make blacks "the kind of people nobody would have any pity for," and thereby shed whatever responsibility they might otherwise have for ameliorating racial injustice.

Margaret uses the term *genocide* to characterize the intentions of the powerful. Where participants in other discussions failed to use the term, they managed nevertheless to convey its meaning:

Group: Pleasant Street
Cast:

Sheila, an administrative aide and college graduate, in her mid 40s.
Sharlene, a teacher with a graduate degree, in her mid 30s.

   Sheila: I have this philosophy that I say it's all part of a plan—
            and the people get scared when I say that.
Sharlene: I agree. I agree.
   Sheila: It's all part of a plan: How do you do away with a race of
            people without a law or anything? You let them kill off
            each other.
Sharlene: Because if it wasn't part of a plan they couldn't congre-
            gate like that in any other neighborhood, the way they
            do here on the corners and stuff. So I really agree with
            you.

Sheila points to the apparent tolerance of the police for street corner drug dealers as evidence of a genocidal plan. And Sharlene asks rhetorically, "How do you do away with a race of people without a law or anything? You let them kill off each other."

The other two incidences of this type of discourse were less fully developed. In one case speakers charged that drugs come "essentially" from the offices of the governor and the mayor. In the other, Alice, whom we first met in Chapter 3 (see p. 52), identified the media as the external agent bent on repressing blacks.

Group: Longwood Road

[In response to question 2:]

   Alice: In general I would say—see—I don't think that violence
            has really gotten any worse. I think the publicity they show
            on the black folks has gotten enhanced more. I don't think
            that it's really that enormous. I think that the media por-
            trays us to be worse and that it's on the increase to try to
            keep us in check—to keep whatever going—I mean—I
            don't know—the whole ghettoized system going.

Rebuttal Displays

There were no direct rebuttals of the charge that the criminal justice system routinely operates in a racist fashion. But speakers in five white and two black groups implicitly rejected the frame's relevance to the Stuart case. One type of rebuttal argument pointed out that Willie Bennett was "no saint" and hence his treatment by the police was at least understandable. Both rebuttals in black groups consisted solely of this observation. It was also expressed in three white groups, but in each case in combination with a more general defense of the police.

The more general defense, advanced in varying degrees of detail in the five white groups, insisted that police reaction to Carol Stuart's murder was reasonable given what the officers knew and the pressures under which they were operating. For example, consider this excerpt from the Maple Street group:

Cast:

Eve, a teacher with a graduate degree, in her 60s.
Maynard, a bank analyst with more than a college degree, in his early 60s.
Diane, a teacher with a graduate degree, in her early 40s.

> Eve: I think that particular case—the reaction—Charles Stuart didn't accuse a particular person that fit the description. So it was only natural that they would look to the black community because it wasn't that they were saying it was a black person, *he* had identified it as a black person. So therefore I don't see anything wrong with the fact that they went to the black community . . .
>
> [A few paragraphs down in the transcript:]
>
> Maynard: I don't blame the police for what happened. I'm sure that the papers love to play it up, but when you have to do something fast you have to do it fast . . .
>
> Diane: Plus, I think there was tremendous pressure on the police department—
>
> Unknown: Sure, absolutely.
>
> Diane: —the nature of the incident. They had to get, you know, they were under a lot of pressure, and I think people nowadays want instant solutions. They want that guy caught—that day! They're not prepared to wait for weeks while the police solve the case.
>
> Unknown: Right!

In two groups, speakers argued that were the "situation reversed," police reaction would have been the same. We encountered an instance of this argument above, in the excerpt from the Jacob's Lane group.

Two other rebuttals deserve quick mention. A speaker in a mixed group argued that critics of the police "throw out the baby with the bath water" and that the problem is limited to a few "rotten apples." And a speaker in a white group referred to the videotape of the King beating, but in order to argue that what "you see on a videotape may look much worse . . . but maybe it's not exactly the way it's shown."

Frame-Neutral Discourse

Of course, the Stuart question did not require a response in terms of the frame *Racist System*. The question was intentionally rather open-ended and engendered a wide variety of responses. Before concluding, we should review some of the frame-neutral discourse sparked by the question.

First, speakers in 11 groups responded with criticism for an allegedly bungled police investigation. Participants noted a variety of facts that ought to have tipped off the police to Charles Stuart's culpability. In one speakers words, "They forgot the first rule of law enforcement: the husband should have been the first suspect."

Second, speakers in 14 groups confessed that they were "taken" by Charles Stuart's ploy "hook, line and sinker." This discourse had a confessional quality to it, but the speakers were quick to note in self-defense the compelling nature of the "stereotype" of the black male criminal:

Group: Holyoke Street
Cast: (See p. 83)

Ellen: It was so clever for Charles Stuart to think of that, you know, that it attached such a fear that was already present that a black male would jump into your car and kill you in the middle of Boston. And it was something so basic to so many people that they were just, you know, obsessed with it. And then when it came out that it was actually a domestic thing—violence against a woman—that was sort of masked in the idea that "Oh! Thank goodness it wasn't really a black man that did this." You know? And it was like "Oh it was this crazy man." But again, it was still a husband killing his wife, being violent against his eight-months pregnant wife. And that in itself is so horrific, but that isn't the big fear here. The fear was racial and not about gender—that whole issue is kind of thrown out once we realized it wasn't a racial episode.

Third, speakers in two white groups and eight black commented that the Stuart case revealed just how racist the city of Boston is. In the black groups these comments often included comparisons of Boston to the South (in the latter, white people "don't treat you like very good and then stab you in the back") and were frequently accompanied by personal experience narratives about racism. While it is important to note that brief comments on the persistence of racism could be heard in two white groups, these comments were *not* expressions of *Racist System*. They were offered as commentary on racial attitudes of people in general, not as commentary on crime or its control.

Finally, speakers lauded the creation of a scholarship fund by Carol Stuart's family for Mission Hill youth (5 white groups and 1 black); criticized the media for "sensationalizing" the Stuart episode (10 groups); and lamented the effect the case has had on the reputations of Mission Hill and the City of Boston (11 groups).

CONCLUSION

Media Violence was the least successful of the five frames. This may simply be an artifact of the research design; the frame is the only one that was not triggered in the discussions by a statement or a question. Two factors lead me to suspect that this is not the case: First, the other frames appeared in most of the discussions in either positive or negative form *prior to being triggered*. Second, *Media Violence* was not only faint in the conversational discourse, it was also nearly invisible in the sample of op eds.

In spite of its inconspicuousness in both the op eds and the discussions, we should note that there were no rebuttal displays of *Media Violence*. The frame apparently has no negative form and indeed is virtually a consensus perspective on crime.

Turning to *Racist System,* we first observe that discourse expressing the frame was difficult to locate in the discussions of white groups. It appeared in weak form in four discussions but in strong form in just one—and there only through a passing reference to Rodney King. *Rejections of Racist System,* appearing in five white discussions, were in fact much more common.

African American participants, on the other hand, spoke readily about abuses by the police and racism in the society. Indeed, the notions that police harass members of minority groups and that Boston is a very racist city were expressed in just about every black group and were unchallenged: they are common places. But it is important to recognize that these notions concerning racism seem to the conversationalists to be irrelevant, for the most part, to an understanding of *crime*. In virtually no case did a participant charge that crime is actually *encouraged* by police harassment or overincarceration of blacks, as a labeling theorist would contend. In only one case did a speaker suggest that specifically racial barriers to achievement, such as segregation in housing and education or discrimination in hiring, might be a source of crime.

The one glaring exception to this observation concerns discourse on a putative conspiracy against inner-city blacks. This argument has no analog in the op ed sample; perhaps its absence from the public discourse accounts for its generally vague nature in the discussions (cf. Sasson, 1995). But talk of conspiracy reveals an apparently widespread sentiment that powerful white people are knowingly responsible for the guns and drugs in black neighborhoods.

We are now ready to move from description to explanation. In Chapters 7 and 8 we explore the sources of popular consciousness about crime.

NOTE

1. The question was not asked in one of the mixed group's discussions, as the interview had already run overtime before the question was reached. The data reported on *Racist System* is thus based on 19 discussions.

7

RESOURCE STRATEGIES AND
FRAME PERFORMANCES:
A CONSTRUCTIONIST
EXPLANATION

What determines popular consciousness about crime? This chapter develops a constructionist explanation. It begins by discussing the limitations of four common models for making sense of popular beliefs about crime. It then describes the principles of an alternative, constructionist approach. Finally, it applies those principles to the discussions to generate the first part of a more satisfactory, constructionist explanation for popular consciousness about crime.

Analysts attribute popular beliefs about crime to the psychodynamic process of displacement, enduring cultural themes, the "implicit ideology" of the criminal justice system and the messages communicated through the mass media. We examine these disparate explanations in turn.

1. *Displacement.* Gordon (1990:161) argues that punitive attitudes toward criminals can derive from social stresses that have little to do with crime.

> People whose material well-being is deteriorating, or who equate social change with the disruption of cherished values, or who feel their voices are not heard in important public debates, may displace their anger and frustration onto the "undeserving," however defined.

This, in Gordon's view, is precisely what occurred in the 1970s and 80s. In the earlier period, the student and civil rights rebellions seemed to working people to flaunt the values of respectability and patriotism. In the later, stagnant wages and growing economic insecurity supplied new sources of anger and resentment. These "structural discontents" were readily channeled, in part by enterprising politicians, into punitive attitudes toward the undeserving, especially criminals.[1]

2. *Enduring Cultural Themes.* Scheingold (1984) argues that the strength of "volitional criminology" (see Chapter 1) derives from a potent bit of American culture that he terms the "myth of crime and punishment." The myth holds that criminals are "predatory strangers," fundamentally different from the rest of us, and eagerly "awaiting their opportunity to attack persons and property."

> This frightening image triggers off a second and more reassuring feature of the myth of crime and punishment: the idea that the appropriate response to crime is punishment. Punishment is both morally justified and practically effective. (p. 60)

The myth derives its strength in part from the twin themes of vigilantism and individual responsibility, both "deep-seated" in American history and culture. But perhaps more importantly, it constructs the problem in a manner that is reassuring. If offenders are readily recognizable and punishment an effective solution, then crime is not so troubling an issue after all. "In effect," Scheingold writes, "the myth of crime and punishment is a simple morality play, a contest between good and evil, with the odds strongly in favor of the good" (1991:21). In contrast, when crime is constructed in structural terms, it becomes everybody's responsibility and the possibility of a "quick fix" disappears.

3. *Criminal Justice Messages.* Reiman (1990) argues that people learn to think about crime by observing the routine operation of the criminal justice system.[2] Thus, the justice system can be said to "broadcast a message" concerning the nature of crime; this message is the system's "implicit ideology." What message does our justice system broadcast? First, by punishing individuals for their offenses, the system "implicitly conveys the message that the social conditions in which the crime occurred are not responsible for the crime" (1990:124). Thus people learn from the everyday operation of the courts that crime is a matter of *choice* rather than a consequence of unjust social arrangements. Second, because (in Reiman's view) the laws criminalize and the courts punish the socially harmful activities of the poor while largely ignoring the more harmful activities of the rich, the criminal justice system teaches that the principal threat to the well-being of middle Americans comes from "those below them on the economic latter, not those above" (p. 130).

4. *Mass Media Messages.* Elias (1993) attributes popular law and order attitudes, at least in large measure, to the influence of the mass media. To discover what messages the news media communicates to the public about crime, he examined all of the crime stories appearing in the newsweeklies *Time, U.S. News and World Report,* and *Newsweek* between 1956

and 1991. The newsweeklies, he discovered, express all of the key features of the "law and order" perspective. In Elias's words:

> Rather than examining whether something might be wrong with our laws, our society, or our fundamental institutions, the newsweeklies conceptualize crime as an entirely individualized problem: Everyone has the opportunity to avoid becoming a criminal. It is the individual's choice, except, of course, for those irretrievably evil people among us who must simply be put away. How, then, can we prevent crime? According to the newsweeklies, we must provide endless resources to law enforcement, abandon rights technicalities that handcuff the police, toughen our penalties and build more prisons. (1993:13)

The message is so uniform, Elias argues, because of media reliance on government officials and conservative crime control experts. These news sources, in turn, derive political benefit from promoting the "law and order" interpretation of crime.[3]

What are we to make of these divergent approaches to the question of popular consciousness about crime? The difficulty with the psychodynamic approach is that it can't be empirically demonstrated. How can we tell if a generation of Americans are displacing their frustration over economic decline onto criminals and crime? Diagnosing displacement in a clinical setting can be a dubious venture; diagnosing a generation's neuroses all the more so. At the same time, in psychoanalytic theory culture is a reaction-formation at the level of the collectivity; it develops as a means of managing widely dispersed psychic stress (Jay, 1976). To the extent that this is so, culture can serve as an empirical indicator for a group's underlying psychodynamic processes. In the interest of remaining squarely within the constructionist paradigm, I will keep my focus in what follows on the cultural (i.e., media discourse and popular wisdom) sources of consciousness about crime. In the concluding chapter, however, I will speculate about psychodynamic processes that might inform and shape this culture.

The remaining models present two problems. First, each privileges a single factor as decisive in shaping consciousness about crime without recourse to evidence against a similarly important role for the others. Second, each treats "effects" (of culture, media and criminal justice messages) as universal outcomes rather than outcomes contingent upon group membership. While media discourse is surely an important resource for making meaning on crime, its effects depend not only on media content but also on the background characteristics and predispositions of audiences (Gamson et al., 1992; Neuman et al., 1992; Lewis,

1991). Likewise, general cultural themes provide resources for thinking about crime. But culture also exists at the level of subculture and in the form of popular wisdom (Gamson, 1992). Thus the culture available to a white professional for making meaning on crime will not necessarily be the same culture available to a working class African American. Finally, even the "implicit messages" conveyed by the criminal justice system differ depending on the structural position of the group. Ghetto dwellers experience the police and the courts in a manner that is distinct from suburbanites (Chambliss, 1994; Anderson, 1990).

Constructionist theory, in contrast, holds that people make meaning out of whatever ideational resources they find handy as a consequence of living within a particular social milieu (Gamson 1988, 1992; Gamson and Modigliani, 1989; Neuman et al., 1992; Gubrium, 1993; Swidler, 1986; Gusfield, 1981; Lewis, 1991). It thus satisfies Morley's (1986:40) ambition to "formulate a position from which we can see the person actively producing meanings from the restricted range of cultural resources which his or her structured position has allowed them access to."

Applied to the question of frame performance in the discussions, constructionist theory posits the following: The most successful frames will be those most readily conjured by discussion participants, given the resources available to them on account of their particular social locations. The explanatory task would then be to show that discussion participants had at their disposal ample resources to conjure the most successful frames (*Faulty System* and *Social Breakdown*) but not the others. This approach promises an explanation for frame performance that would be at once comprehensive in scope and sensitive to group differences. On the down side, it also promises an explanation with somewhat less explanatory power than its rivals. Indeed, saying that people make meaning out of the resources they find available for that purpose has the ring of a truism. And explanations derived from the theory seem likely to come out sounding more like descriptions of *how* people think rather than explanations for *why* they think in one way rather than another. What the constructionist theory needs is a set of hypotheses concerning the relative importance of various types of resources and resource combinations.

My intention in this chapter and the next is to develop one such hypothesis. At the same time, I also hope to provide a satisfactory explanation for frame performance in the discussions. I borrow mostly from William Gamson's (1992) recent work because it moves beyond general constructionist claims to offer the seeds of a more powerful explanatory theory.

GAMSON'S CONTRIBUTION TO CONSTRUCTIONIST THEORY

Gamson examined a sample of peer group discussions about issues in the news to discover the circumstances under which people express elements of a "collective action frame"—a quality of consciousness supportive of social movement participation. Discussion participants were regarded as having expressed such a frame when, with respect to a particular issue, they expressed feelings of injustice, collective identity and agency. For example, when on the issue of affirmative action, black participants expressed outrage over the persistence of racial discrimination, identified themselves as part of a collectivity (i.e., African Americans, black people), and discussed ways to reignite the civil rights movement, they were coded as having expressed a full-fledged collective action frame.

Gamson's argument concerning the wellsprings of collective action frames is a bit complex. He argues that in constructing meaning people draw upon three types of ideational resources: popular wisdom, experiential knowledge and media discourse. He further distinguishes three types of *resource strategies* that conversationalists use to arrive at shared frames. *Personal strategies* are those that combine popular wisdom with experiential knowledge. *Cultural strategies* are those that combine popular wisdom with media discourse. *Integrated strategies* are those that combine all three types of resources. *Integrated strategies* are the key to Gamson's analysis as it is they that tend to produce collective action frames. Gamson explains this tendency by noting that *integrated strategies* combine knowledge that is valued because it is "direct . . . relatively unmediated" with knowledge that is valued because it is widely shared (p. 126). In other words, by matching personal and cultural resources, discussion participants combine the authority and depth of emotion associated with first hand experience with the knowledge—rooted in familiarity with the media discourse—that what is true for me is also true generally.

A CONSTRUCTIONIST EXPLANATION FOR
CRIME DISCOURSE

We can extrapolate from this insight into collective action frames to generate three propositions relevant to our interest in issue frames:

1. Where people have at their disposal a "full spectrum" of resources (media discourse, popular wisdom, experiential knowledge) that can be integrated into a coherent frame, they will tend to make relatively strong arguments on behalf of that frame.

2. Where people have at their disposal a restricted spectrum of resources that can be used to conjure a frame, they will tend to remain silent or make relatively weak arguments on behalf of that frame.

3. Issue frames that prove most successful in group discussions will typically be those conjured through a full spectrum of resources.

The three propositions are obviously closely related, but only the third can be directly tested given the nature of this study. I will refer to it as the "full spectrum" hypothesis.

If the "full spectrum" hypothesis is valid, then we would expect to find that the groups frequently integrated resources when conjuring *Faulty System* and *Social Breakdown* (the most successful frames) but less frequently when conjuring *Blocked Opportunities* (among the least successful). Additionally, we would expect to find that black but not white groups integrated resources when conjuring *Racist System*.

To see if this was the case, I coded the transcripts for resource-use in the context of discussions of the various frames (except *Media Violence,* which did not generate enough discourse to warrant inclusion at this level of analysis). To maintain consistency in the interest of theory building, I used the same working definitions as Gamson (1992:117–34).

Definitions

Experiential knowledge was thus defined as all stories told by participants about personal experiences or those of their family members. Such *personal experience narratives* are typically shared to make a point and hence to conjure a frame. Recall that in Chapter 3 we considered several stories about growing up poor (see, for examples, the speeches of Clara and Alice). These stories were told by participant's to make the point that poverty, per se, does not cause crime. They were thus told to rebut the frame *Blocked Opportunities.*[4]

Of course, one's personal experiences have no inherent meaning and can be used for multiple purposes. I might interpret being mugged by a teenager, for example, as evidence that police and courts need to crackdown, or as evidence that the city needs to expand its juvenile recreational facilities. But there are limits on the range of meanings I can persuasively attach to my first-hand experiences; as a white person, for example, I cannot persuasively draw upon personal experience to make a point about what it feels like to be a target of racism. (As a Jew, I can draw upon my experiences of antisemitism to make claims grounded in empathy, but such claims would carry less weight than those grounded in first-hand experience.) Within the range of plausible meanings, how personal experiences are ultimately interpreted is largely determined by the nature of other available resources, especially media discourse and popular wisdom.

Media discourse is introduced into conversation in two ways. First, speakers can directly refer to a news item or bit of information gleaned from the mass media, as when Alex tells of a "girl on the news" who said "I can do anything I want 'til I'm 18 . . . because I'm underage" (see Chapter 4). Second, speakers can make use of public figures, catchphrases, or spotlighted facts that are part of the public discourse on crime. For example, discourse that mentions Rodney King draws upon a figure who is deeply implicated in the public discourse on policing. Such discourse typically occurs within the frame *Racist System*. Accordingly, references to King were treated as uses of media discourse to conjure (in a positive or negative fashion) *Racist System*.

Similarly the public discourse on crime is rife with catchphrases and slogans. These, too, tend to be properties of particular frames. When a speaker laments a jail's "revolving door," she is drawing upon a slogan deeply embedded in the public discourse on crime—and she is keying the frame *Faulty System*. Accordingly, use of this slogan was treated as an instance of media discourse in support of *Faulty System*.

Finally, the public discourse on crime includes a range of "spotlighted facts" that also tend to be properties of particular frames. Such facts (or better yet, *fact claims*) may be part of the experiential knowledge of researchers or criminal justice administrators, but among regular people they are known strictly through their prominence in the mass media (cf. Gusfield, 1981; Mayer, 1992). When, for example, Carol (Chapter 5) argues that "all of our manufacturing jobs . . . go on to Third World countries and there's just not a lot of upward mobility for people who want to work at minimum wage," she is drawing upon spotlighted facts that are part of the public discourse. More specifically, these facts are properties of *Blocked Opportunities* and were used in the discussions to conjure that frame.[5]

Popular wisdom is the most commonly used resource, but also the one around which it is most difficult to draw boundaries. The term refers to popular beliefs about the way the world works. These beliefs frequently enter conversations through maxims, rules of thumb, Biblical sayings and analogies to everyday life situations. On the continuum that extends from cultural resources (media discourse) to personal resources (experiential knowledge), popular wisdom is in the middle. In Gamson's words, popular wisdom is an amalgam of personal and cultural. On the one hand, it embodies the lessons of personal experience. One's experiences take on meaning by being linked to these rules of thumb. They help to transform the unique experience of different individuals into a bit of popular wisdom that invokes others' similar experiences. . . . Popular wisdom is also part of the media discourse on these issues. Analogies to everyday life and popular maxims are often invoked to make abstract frames more immediate and concrete. (p. 126)

When Vanessa (Chapter 3) argues that "focusing . . . on putting these people in jail, *it's like closing the door after the horse is gone*," she is drawing on a bit of popular wisdom to rebut *Faulty System*. More examples of popular wisdom and the other resources will follow, so without further delay we turn to the question of resource-use in the discussions.

Resource-Use Patterns in the Discussions

As Gamson notes (1992:129), popular wisdom is ubiquitous in everyday talk. Testing of the "full spectrum" hypothesis therefore requires that we analyze only use of the other, more scarce resources. Figure 7.1 describes the results of such an analysis. Fifteen groups (75%) integrated media discourse and experiential knowledge when conjuring *Faulty System* and 15 when conjuring *Social Breakdown*. But just one group (5%) managed to integrate these resources when conjuring *Blocked Opportunities* (this in spite of the fact that *Blocked Opportunities* was expressed in a positive fashion by at least one participant in 85% of the discussions). Similarly, three black (33%) but no white groups integrated resources to

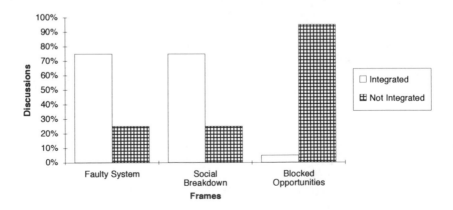

Figure 7.1.   Resource strategies.

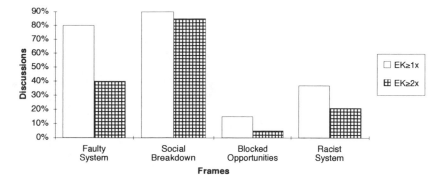

Figure 7.2. Experimental knowledge in the discussions.

conjure a strong version of *Racist System*. The hypothesis is therefore amply supported by the data; the issue frames that proved most successful in the discussions were also those typically conjured through a full spectrum of resources. I want to stress that these patterns need not have obtained. We might imagine a state of affairs in which a frame would perform strongly in discussions while typically being conjured through either a personal or a cultural strategy, or even through popular wisdom alone. However, as the "full spectrum" hypothesis predicts, discussion participants preferred the frames that enabled them to combine knowledge that is valued because it is known first hand with knowledge that is valued because it is widely shared.

Why were the groups typically able to integrate resources when conjuring *Faulty System* and *Social Breakdown* but not when conjuring *Blocked Opportunities*? Why were several black but no white groups able to integrate resources to conjure *Racist System*? Figures 7.2–7.5 suggest the

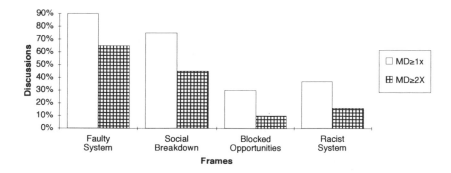

Figure 7.3. Media discourse in the discussions.

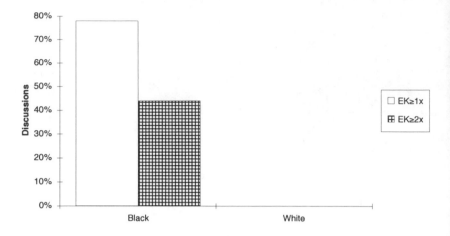

Figure 7.4.   Experiential knowledge on racist system, by race.

beginnings of an answer. The figures describe the number of discussions
in which participants drew upon experiential knowledge and media discourse, respectively, to conjure each of the crime frames. The white bars
describe the number of discussions in which the resource was used once;
the cross-hatched bars the number in which it was used twice or more.
(Note that in Figures 7.3–7.5 the bars for *Racist System* count only media
discourse used to bolster *strong* versions of the frame.)[6]

What these figures show is that the participants apparently had plentiful resources—both cultural and personal—at their disposal for conjuring *Faulty System* and *Social Breakdown* but few for conjuring *Blocked*

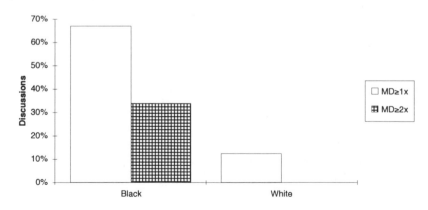

Figure 7.5.   Media discourse on Racist System, by race.

Opportunities. (The latter frame was in fact frequently conjured through popular wisdom exclusively). Similarly, black but not white groups apparently had plentiful resources—cultural and personal—at their disposal for conjuring *Racist System.*

If we compare the cross-hatched bars on Figures 7.2 and 7.3, we do find some noteworthy differences. Experiential knowledge to support *Social Breakdown* was apparently more plentiful than media discourse. And media discourse to support *Faulty System* was apparently more plentiful than experiential knowledge. It also seems that media discourse to support *Blocked Opportunities* was more plentiful than experiential knowledge.

In the remainder of this chapter I describe some of the types of experiential knowledge, media discourse and popular wisdom used to conjure the crime frames. In the following chapter I ask why these resources and not others were available to participants for making meaning on crime.

Experiential Knowledge

The experiential knowledge typically used to bolster *Faulty System* consisted of narratives about encounters with either the police or the courts. Several participants apparently knew the outcomes of cases that personally affected them. For example:

Dean Avenue

Jane: A life sentence is only something like seven years, nine years.

Unknown: Give me a break!

Jane: I'm serious.

Susan: The guy that gets sentenced—All right, our house was broken into, all right? The guy got 30 years. He was out in three.

Peter: He made a deal.

Others reported on delayed police response to 911 calls, neighborhood drug operations tolerated in spite of frequent complaints, and sightings of officers "schmoozing with construction workers." One woman reported on a trial for which she served as an alternate juror:

School Street

Janice: The young man whose trial I sat in on . . . this young man was sentenced to three years and [the judge] *suspended* the

> sentence for this young man. Now he was caught with the smoking gun and the bullets. They chased him and another one—but it was the judge! It's the judges! It's the judiciary system!

The kind of experiential knowledge most frequently used to key or bolster *Social Breakdown* consisted of comparisons between prevailing neighboring and child-rearing practices and those the speaker remembered from her childhood. In some cases speakers recalled their parents as "loving" and "supportive." But in most, parents and neighbors were recalled as strict disciplinarians, albeit affectionately. We encountered several examples of these narratives in Chapter 5 (see, for examples, the speeches of Martin, Alex and Sam). They were told to make a point: Contemporary parents and neighbors, because of their reluctance to demand proper behavior, bear responsibility for delinquent children. Were today's community members as responsible and demanding as their forebears, the problem of crime would be much diminished.

We have also already encountered an example of experiential knowledge used to support *Blocked Opportunities*. In Chapter 3 we heard Charles recall that as a young man he could easily find work at O.J.'s Car Wash or Rothstein's Flower Distributors: "I didn't have to turn to crime to feed myself or to feed my family." But the big news here is how rare it was for participants to use experiential knowledge to conjure this frame. While *Blocked Opportunities'* performance was considerably weaker than either *Faulty System* or *Social Breakdown*, recall that its key elements were expressed by at least 1 participant in 17 of the 20 discussions. But in only 3 of these did speakers draw upon their personal experiences in support of the frame.

Interestingly, speakers in nine discussions introduced experiential knowledge to rebut *Blocked Opportunities* and in five discussions they did so more than once. The experiential knowledge used most frequently in these rebuttal displays consisted of narratives about growing up poor. We encountered examples of these narratives in Chapter 3 (see, for examples, the speeches of Clara and Alice). Their logic is straightforward: We grew up poor. If poverty causes crime, why then are we not criminals? An additional example:

Group: Hallibut Square

> *Janet:* I can't buy that because you're poor that you have to be a criminal. I can't buy that. Cause most of us that grew up here on Mission Hill, we were poor.

Other types of experiential knowledge were also introduced to rebut *Blocked Opportunities*. For example, several African American speakers related encounters with drug dealers in which the latter stated their unwillingness to work a regular job. For example:

Group: Concord Street

June:　I was talking to one guy and I said "Why do you guys do this?" You know? "If I found you a job would you—" He's like "No, there *are* jobs." He said to me someone called him for a job and I think it was paying like five dollars or something an hour. He was like "I'm not taking this job." I mean . . . he just picked, he just chose to do this thing. Now he could have chose to go to college or to take the job. Why did he have to pick the crime?

Finally, recall that *Racist System* was conjured in seven of the nine black groups. In *every one* of these groups experiential knowledge was introduced to bolster the frame. Many of the anecdotes were about racism in general rather than racism practiced by agents of the criminal justice system. But these anecdotes were told in order to drive home the point that racism is *pervasive* and hence *necessarily* reflected in the work of the police and the courts. Consider the following example:

Group: Woodman Road

Doris:　The racism in Boston has to be dealt with. It has to be dealt a death blow . . .

Clara:　Yeah but here, from the beginning of time, ever since I can remember, there was racism. When we're dead and gone Doris there's gonna be racism. But you know why? Because people are *ignorant!* Alright? They let the color of somebody's *skin*—you know—and that's wrong. I remember years ago when I lived in Roxbury—all up in here were nothing but white people. Very few black. All from Grove Hall all the way up. And I was up here by Mayflower Street visiting one day and this car full of white kids stopped: "Nigger, what you doin' up here?" Years ago you couldn't come up in this neighborhood—not walking or catching the MBTA [trolley].

Were we to use a more restrictive standard and include only experiential knowledge of a racist justice system, then we would count use of such knowledge in four discussions. An instance of this type of resource use appeared in Chapter 6, in the excerpt from the Pleasant Street group. Recall that Sharlene drew upon her experiential knowledge of open-air drug dealing to bolster a charge of conspiracy: "If it wasn't part of a plan they couldn't congregate like that in any other neighborhood." Another instance of experiential knowledge of a racist justice system could be heard in the Concord Street discussion. Again, the speaker is June:

> *June:* I feel that a white person *can* point and say, you know, that a black person did it. And I have been in a situation where I was with someone, and they was like, "You fit the description of so and so," and I was like "This guy was with me the whole time. What are you talking about?" There's this stigma. Just this stereotype that blacks are like that.

Media Discourse

We begin with *Faulty System*. Direct references to news stories could be heard in 12 groups, making them the type of media discourse most commonly used to bolster the frame. In the context of a discussion of capital punishment, for example, conversationalists in the Dean Avenue group drew upon a sensational news story about a man who apparently cannibalized his murder victims:

> *Eleanor:* They need to *kill* some people—I'm sorry.
> *Susan:* This guy, now, Jeffrey, what's his face?
> *Unknown:* Dahmer.
> *Susan:* He's insane. What person in their sane mind would—
> *Eleanor:* Dahmer may be innocent.
> *Unknown:* Oh no!
> *Unknown:* Oh *please!*
> *Peter:* They caught him with a heart in his fridge!
> *Several:* Auuuugh!
> *Peter:* He had things in the pot Eleanor! You know, he got caught with his hand in the pot!

Similarly, conversationalists in the Peach Tree Lane group recalled both talk-show and *60 Minutes* episodes relevant to their discussion. The telephone to which Margaret refers in the following excerpt was apparently used by a prison inmate to keep track of his drug dealing operation from behind bars:

> *Ertha:* They're too light with them. They smack them on the hand, even give them weekends to have a little get-

together with their wives or their girlfriends. They have
a private room and every doggone thing. Hey! People
dying to get in jail to have the privilege [laughter]. Seen
it on TV. It was on one of the talk shows, you know?
They had their little private time.

Margaret: They're trying to keep riots down, you see. But I think
they should man the prisons. That's what I think. Man
the prisons and let that keep riots down instead of giving them all the privileges that they get. There was a *60
Minutes* on about a telephone [laughter].

Ertha: This guy, wasn't he making all kinds of calls?

Margaret: A million dollars.

Slogans and catch-phrases were used to bolster the frame in seven
discussions. The number would have been much larger had I counted
"slap on the wrist" or a number of similar tropes as forms of media
discourse. In the end I decided to restrict the operational definition for
media slogans to those that are used exclusively to describe the criminal
justice system. Thus I counted as media discourse the participants claims
that prisons have "revolving doors," that crime victims are "victimized
twice," that the justice system protects the rights of criminals but not
those of victims, that the hands of the police are "tied," that offenders
are released on "technicalities," that if "you do the crime you should do
the time," and that no one wants a prison in her "backyard."

Finally, several different kinds of spotlighted facts were introduced
both to support and to rebut *Faulty System*. The latter are not repre-
sented in Figure 7.3 but deserve attention. In two groups speakers commented that the U.S. has the highest incarceration rate in the developed
world, and in one a speaker lamented the impact of mandatory minimum sentences on prison conditions. Spotlighted facts introduced to
support the frame were, of course, much more numerous. Speakers
discussed, for example, early release, plea bargaining, double bunking
("Quadruple bunk 'em!"), electronic monitoring, community service, restraining orders, community policing and "boot camps."

Turning next to *Social Breakdown*, we must immediately deal with a
problem. The most common type of media discourse used in the discussions also proved to be a borderline case. In five discussions speakers referred to "single parent families" or "single mothers." Am I
justified in counting mere use of this trope as an instance of media
discourse? The manner in which it appeared in two discussions led me
to conclude that I am. Consider this evidence: In the following excerpt
Sally is telling the others about her visit to the mother of a boy who set
fire to her shed:

Group: Gordon Road

    Sally: I did go over and talk to the parent. He had no father. I
            don't know what you call them—"one-parent" I guess
            you call it?
   Martha: Single. Single parents.
    Sally: Single parent. And she said she'd take care of him.

Why does Sally grope for just the right phrase? I suspect that she is
aware that a public discourse exists on "single parent" families—one that
she feels is relevant to the issue of crime. By reaching for the proper
phrase she is attempting to render her bit of experiential knowledge
relevant to the public debate.

A second bit of evidence can be inferred from a speaker who gets the
trope wrong: "I came up in a single family home—my father died real
young." This speaker is not describing a quality of her childhood dwell-
ing, so why the fumble? I suspect that the error stems from the speaker's
attempt to appropriate a bit of media discourse that is not quite native.
She too would like to render her experiential knowledge relevant to a
public issue. Had she relied strictly upon the vernacular she might have
avoided the slip, but her story would have also lost much of its value.[7]

The other uses of media discourse were less equivocal. In four discussions speakers decried a crisis in "family values," thus keying a theme
from the 1992 presidential campaign. And in two discussions each,
speakers commented on "babies having babies," "Ozzie and Harriet,"
and Kitty Genovese.[8] Other uses of media discourse were idiosyncratic,
including references to high divorce rates, television dramas and various
news stories.

The media discourse used to bolster *Blocked Opportunities* in every
instance but one consisted of spotlighted facts.[9] Because of the paucity
of qualifying material, I decided to apply the criteria liberally. Thus, I
regarded as a spotlighted fact the simple observation that "kids don't
have jobs," but I drew the line at the less specific claim that "there are no
jobs." In the public discourse on crime, the rate of juvenile unemployment occupies a prominent place, but the same cannot be said for the
claim that no one has work.[10] The spotlighted facts used in the other
discussions were less marginal: Speakers in four discussions attributed
crime—sometimes obliquely—to either Reagan budget cuts, poor day
care and family leave policies, industrial flight, or a minimum wage that
is too low.

Finally, we turn to media discourse used to bolster strong versions of
Racist System. In Chapter 6 I noted that Rodney King was mentioned in
the conversations of five of the black groups. This public figure was the
most frequent type of media discourse used to bolster the frame. David
Duke, another public figure, made an appearance in one discussion.

Other types of media resources included things seen on television and spotlighted facts.[11]

Popular Wisdom

Many analysts of discourse have noted the contradictory nature of popular beliefs. Gamson (1992) observes that competing maxims contribute to different framings of issues. Billig (1987) argues that the "dilemmatic" quality of common-sense is the foundation for arguing and thinking. Edelman (1977) argues that the contradictory quality of meaningful "symbols" and "vocabularies" enable people to identify with contradictory political positions. On crime, also, people express popular wisdom that supports contradictory framings. But not all beliefs are equally resonant. In this section we examine the types of popular wisdom that appeared most frequently in the discussions and seem to be most important to the performances of the various frames. At the outset, however, I concede that the fuzzy boundaries around the concept "popular wisdom" make a rigorous accounting difficult. Accordingly, I will not quantify my findings but offer a strictly interpretive account.

Two types of popular wisdom appear in numerous discussions to bolster *Faulty System*. The first type stresses the importance of deterrence; it maintains that in the absence of punishment, people will violate the rules. Analogies to disciplining children were a common mechanism for introducing this type of knowledge. Consider the following examples:

Group: Concord Street

> [In response to the trigger statement
> (see Appendix B, question 3, statement 1):]

Karen: I'll strongly agree with that, and that's something that Joy and I were just talking about. It's like if—you know—we were talking about teaching in the public schools and how, you know an analogy to that would be if the students knew they were going to be reprimanded for whatever they do wrong, then maybe they wouldn't do it. There has to be consequences.

Group: Meadowbrook Street

Jerry: I believe that if the justice system does not arrest, try, convict and sentence criminals, then they'll take advantage of that fact. So the question is, in answering the question, the question is, do I think that the criminal justice system is doing that job and doing it effectively. And I guess I don't think it is.

[One page down in the transcript:]

Jenny: I always wondered if [prison] was *really* a miserable place to be and they really—you had *no* rights, in a sense, while you're in there, you were really being punished—you know it's kind of like when we were younger and were told to sit in a corner, they didn't let you sit with a television in front of you. You had to sit in a corner and look at nothing so that you knew you didn't want to do it.

But in a few discussions speakers offered popular wisdom with the opposite message:

Group: Morton Road

[In response to the trigger statement:]

Judith: I don't think people specifically do something because they know they can get away with it. There are a lot of things people think of—jeez, I can get away with this, but they know morally, y'know, it's not right so they don't.

The second form of popular wisdom used to bolster *Faulty System* stresses the flaws inherent in all large bureaucratic organizations. Speakers extended their popular wisdom on corruption, nepotism, organizational waste and mismanagement to the particular case of the criminal justice system. Consider the following examples:

Group: Grove Hills Parkway

Ruth: My feeling is that—I used to work for the news. You turn out a program every day and you have to produce stories every day. So you always have to come up with new ideas. It's sort of like a roller coaster that you get on and can't get off, because there is no time to get off of it. So sometimes you find yourself putting stories out there that maybe shouldn't be on the air for whatever the reason. . . . What's going on right now in society is that we're on this roller coaster and we don't have time to stop, reflect, get off, and look and see where it's not working, because every day you have 100 people going to Roxbury Court, you know, being prosecuted for whatever crimes they've committed the night before. So no one has a chance to stop and say "Hey, this isn't working."

Group: Hallibut Square

Phyllis: They have to give some funding to the courts, too, because everybody is just passing the buck. First of all, you don't have any probation officers . . .

> [A few lines down in the transcript:]

Bob: They waste their money on the most stupid—like they redid Copley Square. For what? I thought it was fine just the way it was—

Phyllis: Didn't you love it when they were going to do the park?

Bob: —and the new State House clock? How do you like that, huh?

Turning now to popular wisdom in support of *Social Breakdown*, two types could be heard in multiple discussions. The first insists that in the absence of discipline and proper moral instruction, children will not learn to behave properly. For example:

Group: Gordon Road

Martha: It comes down to these—teach the child right from wrong and what they should do and what they can't do. From when they're very young. Instill in them the way they did it to us. This way, you'll have a chance—at least a 50/50 chance of getting a child to go right, to do the right things. In other words, the Golden Rule, "Do Onto Others." You have to start when they're very young.

In the next excerpt, this bit of popular wisdom is combined with the second type. The latter asserts that children who are either not "kept busy" or not properly supervised tend to get into trouble. We pick up in the middle of a discussion of the public schools:

Group: Fisher Hill Road

Deborah: What about the younger kids with the educational system. We were just talking about the school committee and the mayor and all of that. The school system is poor, inadequate.

> *Unknown:* Very poor.
> *Deborah:* So that certainly contributed. Their interests are not being kept for those five, six hours that they're there. So they walk out of there. Idle hands are the devil's workshop, or something?
> *Georgia:* That's true too, but I don't think that's an offshoot of poverty. I think that's a person's, well, bring it back down to the parents and stuff. If you don't instill certain things in a child no matter what you give them—
> *Deborah:* O.K. I'll go on with that.
> *Georgia:* —I mean, if you don't have standards, you don't have morals, you know—you don't have basic beliefs, everything's open to you. And those are the things I think that have to—that begin in the home at a very young age.
> *Unknown:* Yeah.
> *Georgia:* And I don't think that's governed really by poverty. I've known too many people that have been dirt poor that have overcome so many—
> *Deborah:* Obstacles.
> *Georgia:* —adversity and stuff.

For *Blocked Opportunities,* the most common types of popular wisdom reinforced *rejections* of the frame. Three closely related types seemed to predominate. The first insists that people *freely choose* their own courses of action; it thus rejects all forms of determinism, including biological and economic. Christine's speech in Chapter 3 ("It's a personal choice . . . It's just a choice you make whether you do [crime] or you don't") is an example of this type of popular wisdom—as is June's first speech above in this chapter.

While an essential part of *Blocked Opportunities'* negative incarnation, popular wisdom on the freedom to choose was sometimes expressed to reinforce *Faulty System.* Consider the following comment from a speaker who might well have been channeling the spirit of Cesare Beccaria:

Group: Grove Hills Parkway

> *Ruth:* When I say the criminals, I mean people who've chosen that kind of behavior for themselves, for whatever reason. I don't think people are born criminals. It's just a name we give people—I could be a criminal. People who want to do that, somehow the message does have to get out that, no, this cannot be done easily. The consequences are even more—the price that they're going to have to pay for that activity is gonna be more than what they're willing to pay. Right now I don't think it is that way.

The second type of knowledge insists that the class/race structure in America is sufficiently open to permit upward mobility. This wisdom is often communicated through the trope "You *can* make it." It is present in white and black discussions but seems, on the whole, more central to the latter. Vanessa's speech quoted in Chapter 4 ("If you're a black person there's no doubt that there's racism. . . . You *can* overcome it and that's what you have to teach your children") is one example. Clara's speech in Chapter 5 is another.

The third type of knowledge holds that poor people are no different from the nonpoor, that "they live their life just as normal as everybody else." Logan and Molotch (1987:134) refer to this bit of popular wisdom as the "liberal doctrine" that "we are all the same" (cf. Best 1990). Because the notion that poor people are just like everybody else clashes with the notion that they are disproportionately engaged in crime, this bit of popular wisdom reinforces rebuttals of *Blocked Opportunities.*

Finally, we turn to popular wisdom used to bolster *Racist System.* Two types were important to both strong and weak displays of the frame. The first insists that racism continues to operate in the society. In the discussions it was offered against the hypothetical interlocutor who might charge that the problem has long since been solved. Not surprisingly, this type of wisdom was expressed in eight of the nine black groups but in just two white groups. When Clara (this chapter) insists that:

> When we're dead and gone . . . there's gonna be racism. But you know why? Because people are *ignorant!*

she is drawing upon this type of wisdom.

The second type of popular wisdom used to support the frame asserts that *everyone* fears young black males. In the discussions, this bit of knowledge was used to explain police and popular reaction to the Stuart murder. Speakers typically confessed to buying the "big con job" "hook line and sinker." By offering this confession they succeeded in both lamenting the power of the stereotype and extending a bit of empathy to the police officers charged with mishandling the case. They were able to do so because of the shared notion that *everyone* fears the young black male. In Chapter 6 we listened to Jane describe the stereotype with exceptional insight. In this final excerpt, we hear Peter make much the same argument:

Group: Dean Avenue

> Peter: I really can't sort out clearly the various levels that this situation with Carol Stuart—how it affected me. I do know, for example, that I bought the big con job. I mean, something in my head immediately reacted to the no-

tion. . . . It was a knee-jerk reaction for me because I—
You see it's much easier for me to think of a black guy
over at Mission Hill ripping—making that happen than it
would be if a white guy had done that. Somehow it made
it more believable to me and—

Several: Yeah, that's what he planned—

Peter: —gee whiz, so that there is a stereotype and because I felt
bad that I was victimized by that stereotype too, and it
doesn't mean that I felt any responsibility—I didn't. That
was an individual act. But that's what tripped me up at the
very beginning.

CONCLUSIONS

Why did *Faulty System* and *Social Breakdown* perform so well and
Blocked Opportunities so poorly? Why did *Racist System* perform well
among blacks and poorly among whites? The constructionist analysis
presented in this chapter demonstrates that *Faulty System, Social Breakdown,* and *Racist System* (among blacks) performed well because: (a) participants had ample resources to conjure them ready at hand, and (b) the
available resources were both personal and cultural in nature. The latter
fact synergistically increased the frames' appeal among discussion participants. *Blocked Opportunities* and *Racist System* (among whites), in contrast, performed poorly because participants lacked media discourse and
experiential knowledge to compliment whatever popular wisdom might
otherwise have been available in support of the frames.

Why were ample cultural and personal resources in support of *Faulty
System, Social Breakdown* and *Racist System* (among blacks) available to the
participants for making meaning on crime? Why were resources for
conjuring *Blocked Opportunities* and *Racist System* (among whites) scarce?
We address these questions in the following chapter.

NOTES

1. Scheingold makes a similar argument, albeit in a more cursory
fashion. America's individualistic culture, he writes, "*increasingly* generates the kinds of insecurities that promote a yearning for scapegoats and
synergistically supplies the volitional understandings that make these
scapegoats credible" (1991:173, emphasis in original; for an argument
concerning the role of scapegoating in generating popular fears over
threats to children, see Best, 1990).

2.   Reiman's argument is actually a popularization of Althusser's theory on the functions of the "ideological state apparatuses." See Althusser, 1971.

3.   Beckett (1994a) makes a similar argument concerning media influence on popular consciousness about drugs and crime, but in her view agency lies first and foremost not with the media but with "state elites," especially Republican politicians, who effectively use the media to disseminate their law and order viewpoints (see Chapter 1).

4.   Gamson notes that people also tell stories about friends and co-workers, and that it is difficult to know where to draw the line on what constitutes personal experience. He decided to restrict the operational definition for experiential knowledge to a speaker's stories about herself and her immediate family.

5.   The coding guide (Appendix B) lists, for each frame, the catchphrases, public figures and spotlighted facts treated as media discourse.

6.   Recall that weak displays of the frame charged racial discrimination in the handling of the Stuart case but failed to generalize from it. Strong displays, on the other hand, treated racial discrimination in the justice system as pervasive, a matter of routine practice. Use of media discourse in the former was ubiquitous; but this is uninteresting, as by definition weak displays were those that discussed what was essentially a media spectacle.

7.   The trope "single parent family" was the sole instance of media discourse in just one discussion. The reader who is unpersuaded by my argument can adjust the findings accordingly.

8.   "Babies having babies" describes a public trend. It is thus a spotlighted fact in addition to a catchphrase. Ozzie and Harriet Nelson are characters on a once popular television series depicting a traditional American family. Concerning the symbolic significance of Kitty Genovese, see Chapter 5.

9.   The one exception was use of the term "underclass," which I treated as a catchphrase belonging to the frame.

10.   The reader who is unconvinced should subtract two discussions (10%) from Figure 7.3.

11.   For examples of things seen on television, see the exchange between members of the Fisher Hill group in Chapter 6. For an example of a spotlighted fact, see Margaret's contribution to the Peach Tree Lane exchange, Chapter 6.

8

CULTURE AND EXPERIENCE

The discussion participants apparently had a surfeit of resources at their disposal to conjure *Faulty System* and *Social Breakdown* but not *Blocked Opportunities*. The black participants but not their white counterparts likewise had ample resources to conjure *Racist System*. Why was this the case? What factors govern the availability of ideational resources? Constructionist theory suggests that we examine the participants' social locations, or, to use Morley's (1986) term, their "structured positions" in society. This turns out to be more complicated than at first it might seem. As members of different social classes and races, the study participants occupy distinct structured positions. As Americans, however, they simultaneously share a common national culture and mass media. And as urbanites and members of families—birth families, at least—they share a range of common experiences. In this chapter, we examine the impact of the participants' *common* and *distinct* structured positions in society on the availability of ideational resources for making sense of crime. We begin with the influence of American culture.

CULTURAL THEMES

Gamson (1992) points out that broad cultural themes—what others refer to as cultural values—are one type of raw material from which popular wisdom can be distilled (there are other types; recall that popular wisdom can also be distilled from experience). Among the themes Gamson discusses is *self-reliance*. This core feature of American culture stresses the responsibility of each individual for her or himself. People should stand on their own two feet! If in the gutter, they should pull themselves up by their own bootstraps! *Self-reliance* celebrates the self-made person, the one that perseveres in the face of obstacles and through hard work achieves material success. The 19th Century novels of Horatio Alger played upon and reinforced the salience of *self-reliance* as a core theme in American culture.

We can refer to a second, closely related theme, as *individualism* (Gans, 1988; Bellah et al., 1985; Carbaugh, 1989). In contrast to the emphasis in *self-reliance* on scaling the class structure, *individualism* highlights the importance of individuality, autonomy and free choice. It holds that each person ought to be regarded first and foremost as a unique individual, and only after that, perhaps, as a member of some ethnic group or larger collectivity. It frowns upon demands for conformity by large bureaucratic organizations, be they businesses or governments. And it celebrates personal choices—doing your own thing—in matters of politics and lifestyle. Individuality, autonomy and the freedom-to-choose are valued in their own right, and insofar as they permit individuals to discover and develop their "true" selves.

The themes of *self-reliance* and *individualism* are the stuff of high-school civics lessons, Fourth of July oratory, and political campaign rhetoric. Their resonance, moreover, is not restricted to whites. As numerous analysts (Jhally and Lewis, 1992; Gamson, 1992; Carbaugh, 1989; Gans, 1988) have observed, African Americans are just as committed to the values captured in the twin themes.

Self-reliance and *individualism* are the basis for much popular wisdom expressed in the discussions. The notion that the class structure is open, that those who strive and play by the rules can move up, is rooted in *self-reliance*. The bit of wisdom that says "everyone's the same"—that from a moral standpoint the poor are no different from the nonpoor—derives from *individualism* (i.e., the belief that people ought to be regarded first and foremost as individuals and not as members of groups). And the notion that people freely "choose" crime derives, in part, from the notion that people are responsible for their own welfare (*self-reliance*), and in part from the veneration people attach to the act of choosing (*individualism*). Taken together, these various bits of popular wisdom were central to the strong performance of *Faulty System* and the weak performance of its ideological antagonist *Blocked Opportunities*.

A third theme is what Scheingold (1984, 1991) refers to as the "myth of crime and punishment." As explained in the previous chapter, the deeply rooted myth holds that the threat to our wellbeing stems from "predatory strangers" and that punishment is an "effective and virtuous" response to crime (1991:21). It therefore encourages people to unreflectively conflate crime with punishment, that is, to regard criminal justice solutions to crime as *natural*. The theme therefore provides sustenance to popular wisdom on deterrence; such wisdom, of course, was used to key *Faulty System*.

MASS MEDIA

The mass media supply the spotlighted facts, public figures and catch-phrases that we have termed media discourse. They also play a role in reinforcing particular types of popular wisdom. We need to distinguish, however, between the contributions of various *types* of media. In what follows, we begin with the elite public discourse, and then turn to news and entertainment media.

Public Discourse

The op ed sample is a good index of the elite public discourse on crime. Judging from the analysis presented in Chapters 3–6, Graber (1980—see Chapter 1) is correct in arguing that the public discourse on crime is diverse. But not all frames are equally salient in the public discourse, and differences in frame salience correspond to differences in the use of media discourse in the discussions. To be more specific, recall that *Faulty System* was the dominant frame in the op ed sample and also the frame most frequently conjured in the discussions through use of media discourse (see p. 133). At the same time, *Media Violence* and *Racist System* were the least successful frames in the op ed sample and, together with *Blocked Opportunities*, were also the frames least likely to be conjured in the discussions through media discourse. The sheer volume of public discourse supporting *Faulty System* and *Social Breakdown* was thus likely a factor in determining the availability, among discussion participants, of media discourse for conjuring those frames.

Not only is the volume of public discourse on each frame important, so too is its quality. This is especially evident when contrasting the participants' use of media discourse to bolster *Blocked Opportunities* with their use of media discourse to bolster *Social Breakdown*. The overall performances of the two frames were roughly comparable in the op ed sample, but *Social Breakdown* was frequently introduced in the discussions through use of media discourse while *Blocked Opportunities* was rarely introduced in this fashion. What accounts for this difference? I think the key lies in the fact that the media discourse on *Social Breakdown* features catchphrases and slogans (e.g., "family values," "babies having babies") while the media discourse on *Blocked Opportunities* consists almost exclusively of fact claims. Catchy slogans are simply easier to remember than dry fact claims; perhaps they are also more gratifying to deploy in conversation.

News and Entertainment Media

News and entertainment media reinforce popular wisdom used in the discussions. With respect to the participants' frequent refrain that crime is a matter of free will, Iyengar's (1991) experimental research on television news formats is especially instructive. He distinguishes between two news formats, the "episodic" and the "thematic." The "episodic" form— far and away the most common—treats events as discrete happenings; episodic crime stories, for example, describe isolated instances of murder or mayhem. The much rarer thematic form, in contrast, highlights trends, persistent problems or other larger social phenomena. To test the impact of story format on viewers' attributions of responsibility for social problems, Iyengar exposed experimental and control groups to stories that were systematically altered along the episodic-thematic dimension. He found that stories told in the episodic format encouraged viewers to attribute responsibility for social problems to individuals rather than societal forces. Stories told in the thematic format had the opposite effect. With respect to crime, television news thus cultivates the notion that it is individual criminals and not society who are ultimately responsible. It therefore tends to reinforce the popular wisdom that says crime is a matter of individual "choice."

Together with cop shows such as *N.Y.P.D. Blue, Homicide* and *Law and Order,* crime news also promotes the "myth of crime and punishment." The chain of causality in this case is much more direct. As Lewis (1991:146) notes, by frequent repetition, the mass media can promote associations between discrete phenomena. Both crime news and cop shows focus mostly on criminal investigations, arrests and trials. They therefore reinforce the popular tendency to conflate *crime* and *punishment,* and in this fashion contribute to the popular wisdom on deterrence (cf. Carlson, 1985).

Finally, Jhally and Lewis (1992) argue that prime-time television programs—they examined *The Cosby Show* in depth, but the observation rings true more generally—increasingly eschew stereotypical images of African Americans. Instead, such programs represent social situations in which African Americans hold positions of prestige and power, and in which distinctions of race and class are backgrounded. This sort of representation, Jhally and Lewis contend, obscures the persistence of racism and class barriers in the society and cultivates a naive faith in the possibility of upward mobility. One need not accept their characterization of the "American dream" as an unrealistic "fantasy" in order to appreciate the role of television fiction in cultivating it. And the American dream, as we have seen, is a kind of popular wisdom used to rebut *Blocked Opportunities.*

URBAN AND FAMILY LIFE

In addition to sharing the same national culture and mass media, the participants are all urban dwellers and members of families of one sort or another. These simple biographical facts supply a range of experiences and related popular wisdom that the conversationalists put to use in the discussions.

As contemporary urban dwellers, all have had experiences of various sorts with the criminal justice system. Many, for example, have served on juries, dialed 911 for emergency assistance, or witnessed a police rousting a suspected drug dealer. All have observed police cars cruising their neighborhood and had at least casual encounters with police officers. Of course, such experiences could in theory be used to rebut *Faulty System*. The participants' popular wisdom and media discourse, however, provided little support for such usage. As a result, experiential knowledge of the criminal justice system was mobilized almost exclusively to conjure positive versions of the frame.

As members of families, virtually all of the discussion participants have had a variety of experiences with children (those who do not themselves have children can at least remember once having been a child!). These experiences—and the popular wisdom they have engendered—supplied numerous resources for making sense of crime. For example, they are surely at the root of the widespread notion that children must be supervised and disciplined—at least occasionally—if they are to stay out of trouble.

That the participants recall more discipline having been administered in the past than today is difficult to interpret. Certainly the notion that in the old days parents punished their children more swiftly and harshly is widespread. The working class parents chronicled by Lillian Rubin in her 1975 book *Worlds of Pain* expressed similar views:

> My folks, especially my father, made us toe the line, not like kids today. When my brother got out of line, my father nearly killed him. Actually, I guess I'm not sure how much good it did because he kept getting into trouble. (pp. 31–2)

Whether contemporary parents are correct in their assessment of prevailing parenting practices or simply nostalgic for an idealized past is unclear. But what certainly has changed in the lifetimes of the study participants is the composition and nature of the "typical" American family. Since its heyday in the 1950s, the modern family—male breadwinner, female homemaker, sundry children—has been in steady decline. Emerging in its place, as Stacey (1991) explains, are a hodgepodge of single-parent families and blended household arrangements. The transition to these "postmodern" families is being fueled, in large measure, by rising rates of divorce and out-of-wedlock births.[1] Discussion participants who attributed poor parenting to "family breakdown" or the absence of fathers were thus pointing to a very real social development.

In the final analysis, of course, the fact that the study participants drew upon their personal experiences with families to support *Social Breakdown* and not some other frame is partly due to the nature of the other resources at their disposal. But just as clearly there is something inherent in family life—in general and in this historic moment—that makes its attendant experiential knowledge and popular wisdom especially resonant with *Social Breakdown*.

CLASS AND RACE

Class and race contribute to the pool of resources for making sense of crime by providing subcultural popular wisdom and by shaping typical life experiences. They also influence attentiveness to media discourse and hence its availability as an ideational resource.

Social Class

Social class influences the pool of resources available for conjuring *Blocked Opportunities* and *Faulty System*. Two types of influence can be observed but the more striking of the two can be found only in the subsample of white participants. It turns out that 50% of white participants who graduated college expressed positive versions of *Blocked Opportunities* as compared to 9% of those without college degrees.[2] The same relationship can be observed for negative displays of *Faulty System:* 46% of the white participants who finished college rebutted at least part of that frame as compared to *none* of those without a college degree. It thus appears that for white participants graduating college is practically a necessary if insufficient condition for conjuring either *Blocked Opportunities* or the negative version of *Faulty System*.

Why might this be the case? We begin with the impact of social class on the availability of media discourse. Members of the professional middle class, by virtue of their educational attainment, jobs, and class-culture, are especially attentive to the ongoing political spectacle (Neuman, 1986; Mcombs, Ensiedel, and Weaver, 1991). They are thus more likely than others to be able to make use of relatively obscure media discourse

While positive versions of *Blocked Opportunities* and negative versions of *Faulty System* were present in the op ed sample, they were not expressed through memorable catch-phrases or public figures but rather through comparatively dry, spotlighted facts. Not surprisingly, therefore, it turns out that the participants who expressed these perspectives through use of media discourse were overwhelmingly college graduates.

Another observation can be made, this one with respect to popular wisdom. Derber, Schwartz, and Magrass (1990) argue that a cleavage exists within the ranks of the professional middle class with respect to attitudes on government efforts to reduce poverty. On the one hand are professionals employed in the private sector who tend by a large majority to "show little sympathy for people on welfare" (p. 176). On the other are the academic and public-sector professionals who tend as often as not to support "government intervention or planning to stimulate growth, reduce poverty and pollution, protect consumers and prevent economic breakdown" (p. 180). The distinction between private and public sector professionals is useful: it turns out that 11 of the 13 white participants who expressed positive versions of *Blocked Opportunities* fit into the latter category. They include people who work in the public schools, local government, nonprofit organizations and academia. That these individuals had popular wisdom in addition to media discourse handy to conjure *Blocked Opportunities* is thus likely a consequence of their common occupational subculture.

The second influence of class is less directly observed but seems relevant to black and white participants alike. It stems from the fact that few of the participants are poor or members of the so-called urban underclass (Wilson, 1987). Studies of crime watch mobilizations (Skogan, 1990; Rosenbaum, 1987) demonstrate that participants tend to be homeowners or long-term renters with a stake in their community. This is also true for participants in this study. In Chapter 2, I noted that all of the crime watch groups in the sample were located in relatively stable middle- and working-class neighborhoods, often abutting but always distinct from seriously run-down areas. Moreover, of the 110 participants, only 14 reported household incomes of less than $15,000, while 58 reported incomes of $30,000 or more.[3]

That relatively few conversationalists are poor has an obvious bearing on the resources available to them for making sense of crime: People who are not poor cannot readily draw upon experiential knowledge to bolster *Blocked Opportunities*. But what of the many participants who report having grown up poor? Contrary to what one might expect, these participants did not tend to express empathy for the disadvantaged based on their common experience. But neither did they simply "blame the victim" (Ryan, 1976). Instead, they bore witness to the possibility of making it in spite of injustice and adversity. Apparently the experience of emerging from poverty encourages a view of the class structure as at least partially fluid. (This view, at the same time, is encouraged by the cultural themes of *individualism* and *self-reliance*). Thus, many participants expressed experiential knowledge supportive of the notion that people *choose* their peculiar paths, and that some people *choose* crime. This notion directly contradicts the central argument of *Blocked Opportunities* and hence militates against support for the frame.

There is an implicit assumption in the argument I am making that cannot be examined given the limits of the study sample. I am assuming that in a sample, which included more people who are currently poor, expressions of *Blocked Opportunities* would be more common. Of course, we might still expect to hear statements of faith in the possibility of upward mobility; American culture encourages even the poor to accept responsibility for their plight. But the experiential knowledge of current deprivation likely intrudes in the discourse of those at the bottom of the American class structure. Peer group discussions among poor urbanites could test the soundness of this assumption.

Race

Race proved important with respect to resources used to conjure *Racist System* and certain elements of *Social Breakdown*. We begin with the media discourse and experiential knowledge used to conjure *Racist System*. As noted in the previous chapter, the ideological impact of media discourse is in part a function of the predispositions of audiences (Gamson et al., 1992; Neuman et al., 1992; Lewis, 1991). White and black participants alike were presumably exposed to copious media coverage of the notorious police beating of Rodney King. But whites almost never used King's image as a resource for conjuring *Racist System* while blacks frequently did so. This difference is in part due to differential attentiveness to media discourse. For the African American participants, coverage of the King episode and its aftermath was important and hence memorable. They therefore had King, as a bit of media discourse, ready at hand when an opportunity to deploy him arose.

The African American participants also keyed strong versions of *Racist System* with experiential knowledge of racism in the criminal justice system. Their first-hand experiences of bigoted cops echo the rich ethnographic literature on policing practices in black neighborhoods (see Chambliss, 1994; Anderson, 1990). They also made ample use of experiential knowledge concerning racism in general—and popular wisdom rooted in that knowledge—to conjure the frame. Among whites, experiential knowledge of racism is much more restricted and popular wisdom on the subject more likely to be contested. No wonder, then, that black participants had those resources more readily available to conjure *Racist System.*

This analysis sheds light on a paradox. How is it that many African American participants denounced the criminal justice system for racism, on the one hand, while they decried its alleged leniency and called for harsher punishments, on the other? The paradox is resolved when we see that they had ample resources—personal as well as cultural—to support both *Faulty System* and *Racist System.* That the frames seem mutually contradictory is a problem that can presumably be worked out by individual thinkers upon demand. As Billig (1987) points out, what social psychologists term "cognitive dissonance" is really a rhetorical challenge more than anything else. Since I didn't ask the participants to reconcile the apparently dissonant discourses, I cannot report how they would do so.

Turning now to resources used to conjure *Social Breakdown,* we note that white and black participants alike drew upon experiential knowledge of their childhood communities to lament the decline of responsible neighboring. As noted in Chapter 5, however, this discourse was especially rich in the black groups. The African Americans recalled their neighbors helping out in various ways and sharing in disciplining "all of the neighborhood kids." These days, they argued, irascible parents and unpredictable youth have made people too frightened to intervene.

Like their discourse on racist policing practices, the black groups' observations about community life echo the ethnographic literature. Elijah Anderson (1990), for example, writes about the decline of mentoring relationships between older black males ("old heads") and neighborhood boys. Similarly, Patricia Collins (1990) laments the decline of collective parenting practices that she terms "other-mothering." The black groups' discourse on the decline of good neighboring thus is rooted in the distinct history of contemporary African American neighborhood life.

The black groups' discourse on parenting practices also differs in certain respects from that of the white groups. Recall that many African American participants argued that laws against child abuse discourage proper discipline and are therefore *criminogenic.* This apparently widespread sentiment seems rooted, in part, in their experiential knowledge of children that were removed from their parents homes by overzealous social workers. But in only one or two discussions did speakers introduce direct experiential knowledge of this phenomenon. Instead, the typical mechanism by which it entered the discussions was popular wisdom. It seems that this piece of the collective experience of African Americans has been transformed into a kind of cultural common-place.

Another explanation focuses on African American culture more generally. Opinion research by political scientists Robert Smith and Richard Selzer (1992:42) indicates that across a range of "social issues" including "the role of women in modern society, abortion, homosexuality, and school prayer," African Americans are more conservative than whites. It seems likely that this cultural conservatism extends to attitudes on child-rearing techniques. Popular wisdom on the relationship between discipline and crime thus seems to reflect a broader subcultural orientation.

CONCLUSION

The constructionist explanation developed in this and the previous chapter is illustrated in Figure 8.1. Cultural themes, media discourse, family and urban life, and race and class, each influence the contents of the pool of resources available to discussion participants for making sense of crime. The contents of this pool of resources, in turn, determine whether participants will pursue a cultural, personal or integrated resource strategy when discussing each of the crime frames. Finally, the nature of the strategy the participants pursue governs frame performance; integrated strategies result in strong performances; cultural and personal strategies in relatively weaker performances.

The key to understanding popular constructions of crime therefore lies not only in the relative volume of, but also in the relationships between, available resources, as the "full spectrum" hypothesis predicts. With respect to crime, the pool includes both ample *and diverse* resources for conjuring *Faulty System* and *Social Breakdown*. Participants were thus readily able to integrate the personal and the cultural in conjuring these frames, and therefore made the strongest arguments on their behalf. The participants were certainly competent to conjure *Blocked Opportuni-*

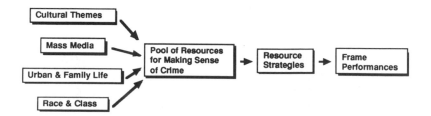

Figure 8.1.   Frame performances in the discussions.

ties, but the resources for doing so are more scarce. For any given group, they were less likely to be both handy and available in diverse form.

Perhaps an analogy will help drive home my general theoretical argument. Imagine you've invited guests to dinner but cannot decide whether to prepare an Italian, Chinese or Mexican meal. You go to the market to find out which meal would be easiest to prepare given the foodstuffs set out on the shelves. For a Chinese meal, you find Tofu and soy sauce but no bok choy. For a Mexican meal, you find Taco shells and refried beans but no fresh Jalepenos. Thankfully, the situation with respect to Italian ingredients is altogether different. First of all, the Italian section is huge; whereas the Mexican and Chinese sections occupy only a few feet of aisle space, the Italian section runs almost the full aisle length. Second, the Italian section includes numerous varieties of pastas, sauces, cheeses—everything you could possibly need for a week's worth of complete meals. This settles the matter; you purchase the ingredients and prepare an Italian dinner.

Imagine that the Mexican and Chinese ingredients represent the resources available—in volume and type—for conjuring *Blocked Opportunities* and *Racist System* (among whites), and that the Italian ingredients represent the resources available for conjuring *Faulty System* and *Social Breakdown*, and you get the idea.

In the following chapter we return to the central theoretical questions that framed this study.

NOTES

1. Demographers estimate that as many as two-thirds of recently contracted marriages will end in divorce. With respect to nonmarital fertility, the data are just as striking: Between 1985 and 1988, 40% of children of women who gave birth for the first time were conceived out of wedlock. Among African American women the figure was 79% (Bumpass and Castro, quoted in Stacey, 1991).

2. Twenty-three white participants reported having less than a college degree, 26 a college degree or more and four left the item on the questionnaire blank.

3. Eleven respondents reported household incomes of $15,000–$29,999. Income information is missing for 27 respondents. Most of these left the question on income blank. A few departed the meeting prior to completing a questionnaire. Race differences are not conspicuous when using the upper cut-off point of $30,000 or more, but African American participants were somewhat more likely to leave the question blank.

9

CONCLUSION

Conventional wisdom is not always wrong; in this case, it receives a good deal of support from the data. Let us briefly review the book's central findings, beginning with the elite public discourse.

Faulty System was by far the strongest frame in the op ed sample. Although its conservative subframe, *Leniency*, did not perform that well, its technical subframe, *Inefficiency*, was keyed in a positive fashion in nearly half of the op eds. Recall that *Inefficiency* implies a volitional perspective on crime and prescribes a criminal justice solution; its strong performance is therefore entirely consistent with the notion that media discourse blames crime on individual moral failure and a poorly functioning criminal justice system. At the same time, *Racist System* and *Blocked Opportunities*, the two frames that imply social or structural causes for crime, performed relatively poorly.

Against the temptation to oversimplify, however, we should recognize that all of the frames were visible in the op ed sample and hence that all were "available" in the public discourse. This observation is almost too obvious to deserve mention, but some analysts imply that alternatives to the law and order perspective are altogether absent (Elias, 1993).

Turning to the popular discourse, we see that the conventional wisdom is again supported. This conclusion is occasioned by the strong performances of both versions of *Faulty System* and the relatively weak performance of *Blocked Opportunities*. Most of the discussion participants did indeed argue in favor of a more vigorous and punitive criminal justice system, and most rejected the notion that crime stems from economic hardship or discrimination.

The frame that performed most successfully in the discussions, however, does not attribute crime to criminal justice leniency; rather, it points to moral decline, poor parenting and community disintegration. At first blush, *Social Breakdown* may seem to be a structural interpretaation of crime; its strong showing may therefore seem to pose a challenge to the conventional wisdom. In fact, however, the frame is only structural in its liberal version (that is, when it attributes moral, familial and community decline to economic hardship or racial discrimination). In its neutral version, it does not specify the antecedents of decline; it therefore depicts parents and neighbors, at least implicitly, as moral agents largely responsible for their actions—and thus for whatever crimes their actions engender.[1] In the discussions, this depiction was occasionally made explicit, as when Ruth, of Grove Hills Parkway, observed: "Family disintegration . . . it stems from the individual. . . . We need to get stronger."

Social Breakdown was *almost always* expressed in its neutral version. The frame's strong performance is thus consistent with the conventional wisdom that people regard individuals (and not social arrangements) as principally responsible for crime. Nevertheless, the frame's focus on family and community makes it more amenable than *Faulty System* to reframing in structural terms, as in its liberal version. This fact is missed by analyses that neglect the centrality of family and community in popular constructions of crime. Its significance will be explored below.

In sum, the discussion participants do indeed, to borrow Scheingold's phrase (1991:6), demonstrate an "ingrained aversion to structural criminology." But here too I must caution against the temptation to draw conclusions that are too sweeping. The most noteworthy example of this tendency is *Policing the Crisis* (1978), the encyclopedic study of an alleged "moral panic" over mugging in the United Kingdom. Author Stuart Hall and his associates occasionally suggest that "counter-hegemonic" discourses on crime circulate in English culture. More frequently, however, they insist that on the topic of crime, there is "ideological closure." Against this sort of hyperbole, I note that in my sample of discussions *Blocked Opportunities* was expressed in a positive fashion by at least one speaker in 85% of the groups, and that it performed well among the highly credentialed public sector professionals. Moreover, I also note that *Racist System* performed well in the black groups. While these frames were subordinate to the others in terms of overall performance, they were far from invisible.

CONSTRUCTIONIST THEORY AND ITS LIMITS

To explain frame performance I advanced a refined version of constructionist theory. It demonstrates that analysts who attribute popular thinking on crime to cultural themes (Scheingold, 1984, 1991), the implicit messages of the criminal justice system (Reiman, 1990) and the mass media (Elias, 1993) are not so much wrong as only partly right.

Attributing popular constructions of crime to media influence exclusively is particularly problematic. At a general level, it is true that the frames that enjoyed the most prominence in the op ed sample were also the ones that performed most successfully in the discussions. But against an overly deterministic impression of the significance of this finding, recall that in several instances the media and popular discourses were divergent. *Leniency*, for example, performed relatively poorly in the media sample but was very much in evidence in the discussions. Gamson's hypothesis, offered at the conclusion of *Talking Politics* (1992:180–1), is instructive:

> People who use integrated [resource] strategies are selectively influenced by the relative prominence of media frames, responding to the degree that these frames are consistent with their popular wisdom and experiential knowledge. They are constrained by omissions from media discourse but relatively immune to differences in the relative prominence of visible frames.

Given that *Leniency* is broadly resonant with the popular wisdom and experiential knowledge of many of the discussion participants, it does not really matter that the subframe was relatively inconspicuous in the elite public discourse.

Thus both culture and experience—and the popular wisdom, media discourse and experiential knowledge they supply—are key factors in shaping consciousness. Specifically, I have argued, after the full spectrum hypothesis, that the availability of abundant and diverse (on the cultural-personal continuum) resources in support of *Faulty System* and *Social Breakdown* is responsible for their strong performances in the discussions. (The relative absence of the same with respect to *Blocked Opportunities* explains its relatively weak performance.) Further, I have argued that diversity of resources is important because by integrating the personal and the cultural conversationalists were able to combine the authority of first-hand experience with a mandate to generalize to the experiences of others. Integrating resources thus enabled them to link their biographies to history, and thereby to exercise what C. Wright Mills (1959) called the "sociological imagination."

Like most social phenomena, however, consciousness about crime is *overdetermined*. We should not expect a single theory to provide a total explanation. Constructionist theory highlights the central role of "structured position" in the society and attends to the process of assembling meaning from available resources. At the same time, it backgrounds the significance of *interests, interactional context* and *psychology*. We will briefly explore the significance of each.

Interests.   Because their experiential knowledge and popular wisdom coincide in a depiction of the class structure as basically fluid and open, many participants regard *Blocked Opportunities* as fundamentally at odds with the dominant message they, as parents, want to impart to their children. If upward mobility is possible, then faith in the possibility of "making it" is essential to personal success. Indeed, if we add the caveat "by legitimate means," then it is also essential to avoiding crime. Hence, as parents, many participants regard the determinism implicit in *Blocked Opportunities* as anathema—exactly the wrong message to communicate to children. To encourage young people to strive for personal success— and to dissuade them from crime—it is imperative that they be made to internalize the message "You *can* make it!" This is so whether the obstacles to be overcome derive from class inequality or racial discrimination. Parental interests in the success of children thus militated against support for *Blocked Opportunities*.

Interactional Context. Speakers, both white and African American, seemed eager to avoid stigmatizing African Americans by implying that they are disproportionately involved in crime. In many discussions, this desire seemed to encourage participants to describe crime as a matter of individual choice (and hence not group membership) and to argue that crime is "everywhere" (and hence not concentrated in black neighborhoods—see Chapter 2). The desire to publicly eschew a stereotype commonly regarded as racist thus encouraged expressions of the popular wisdom that "we are all the same." It therefore undermined support for *Blocked Opportunities,* and encouraged support instead for *Faulty System* and *Social Breakdown,* the two frames most compatible with attributions to individual choice.

Psychology. As noted in Chapter 7, Gordon (1991) and Scheingold (1991) argue that popular law and order attitudes are fueled by the psychodynamic processes of displacement and projection. In this interpretation, during the past 30 years the challenges to the traditional status hierarchy posed by movements for social equality (e.g., civil rights, feminism), coupled with increasing economic insecurity among members of the working class, generated widespread anxiety and social discontent. "Does it not stand to reason," asks Scheingold (1991:174), "that bottling up anxieties will eventually engender a good deal of free-floating anger and occasion a search for scapegoats against whom to discharge this anger and through whom to maintain the hollow illusion of control?" Criminals, in this context, have come to represent the agents of social disorder and decline, and punishment has become a preferred strategy for restoring a more congenial social order.[2]

Psychodynamic explanations of this sort are fully compatible with my general findings—although they explain them at an altogether different level of analysis. This is so insofar as such explanations posit strong performances by the frames that enable people to blame crime on individuals rather than abstract social conditions, and that facilitate a demand for harsh punishment. As we have seen, in terms of the frame catalogue developed in this study, this means *Faulty System* (especially its subframe *Leniency*) and—though to a lesser extent—*Social Breakdown*.

POLITICS AND PUBLIC POLICY: THE SIGNIFICANCE OF CRIME

The discourses of the urbanites who participated in this study reflect the most robust findings of survey research, especially the notions that people are critical of the courts and favor harsher punishments for offenders (see Chapter 1). Stinchcombe et al. (1980) demonstrate, however, that punitiveness varies somewhat by region, with its greatest concentration in rural areas and the South (places associated with the "rural hunting culture"). There are thus grounds for believing that the discussion participants as urbanites and northeasterners, are somewhat *less* punitive than the American public as a whole.

What then is the significance of crime's salience on politics and public policy? The conventional wisdom, as discussed in the introduction, maintains that attention to crime benefits conservative politicians and fuels criminal justice expansion. Nothing I have discovered leads me to challenge these conclusions. I would like, however, to reflect on them a bit further.

Conservative Political Successes

Political campaigns in 1994 focused more on crime than any other issue. Candidates nationwide engaged in schoolyard-like contests over who was tougher and more capable of standing up to criminals. Driving the escalating rhetoric, in part, was the bid by "new Democrats," including President Clinton, to appear as tough as Republicans and thereby neutralize the issue. But the Republicans would not be outdone. In Florida, gubernatorial candidate (and son of the former President) Jeb Bush called for corporal punishment of the sort practiced in Singapore. On the television program *Meet the Press,* Texas Senator Phil Graham promised a "real crime bill" that "grabs violent criminals by the throat, puts them in prison, and that stops building prisons like Holiday Inns." And in North Carolina, congressional candidate Fredrick Kenneth Heineman urged that provisions of the North American Free Trade Agreement be used to export U.S. criminals to Mexico "where they can be warehoused more cheaply." Even in Vermont, the state with the second lowest crime rate in the nation, the incumbent Republican senator, Jim Jeffords, attacked his Democratic rival for being soft on crime.

All this overheated campaign rhetoric is probably the best explanation for the salience of crime at a time when crime rates in most places were either steady or in modest decline (Chambliss, 1994). But whatever the explanation for the issue's salience, it is no coincidence that it coincided with massive Republican victories in congressional, gubernatorial and other elections nationwide. Moreover, the issue's effectiveness on behalf of conservatives was not lost on those newly elected or returned to office. Among the first moves of the new congressional leadership was to announce its eagerness to "revisit" the 1994 Crime Bill in order to reallocate money earmarked for "prevention" to more punitive purposes.

As the salience of crime in the race for Vermont's seat in the U.S. Senate indicates, the symbolic politics of crime have a life of their own. In the foreseeable future, conservative politicians will try hard to keep the issue on the public agenda. And judging from the findings I've presented in this book, they will benefit to the extent that they succeed in so doing.

Criminal Justice Expansion

Whether caused by the reality of victimization or the dynamics of the political spectacle, the salience of crime as a political issue will continue to generate demands for an ever larger and more punitive criminal justice system. The high costs of criminal justice operations will likely serve as a brake on these demands but not contain them altogether.

At the federal level, the Crime Bill, if it is not significantly altered by the new Republican-led Congress, will fund the hiring of 100,000 new local police officers and the construction of tens of thousands of new prison cells. It will also ensure, through its "three strikes and you're out" and "truth in sentencing" provisions, that the new prison construction will perpetually lag behind demand for additional cell space.

Such demand will also be sustained by the more than dozen states that have adopted their own versions of the three-strikes legislation. The California Department of Corrections estimates, for example, that California's three-strikes law will cost the state $21 billion for new prison construction and $5.7 billion annually for prison operations. Further, it estimates that the legislation will cause a 275,000 person increase in the state's prison population over the next 30 years (Mauer, 1994).

In addition to expanding in size, there is evidence that the system is becoming progressively more punitive. Overcrowding in the vast majority of state and federal prisons has led to the widespread practice of double-bunking inmates in six-by-ten foot cells designed for one. High tech isolation units modeled after California's notorious Pelican Bay Penitentiary are proliferating nationwide. The State of Alabama has introduced the chain-gang and other states are expressing interest. Death row is now the home for 2,800 inmates and Congress is poised to streamline the process by which they will be executed. And support for rehabilitation programs of just about any sort is at an all-time low.

In addition to benefiting conservative politicians and fueling criminal justice expansion, the salience of crime will likely have at least three other political effects. I would like to briefly touch upon each.

Legitimating Inequality

The salience of crime will likely undermine support for general efforts to improve the circumstances of the urban poor. Let me explain why. The discussion participants view street crime as disproportionately the work of poor people and members of minority groups. If they also interpreted crime as a result of economic inequality, then their perceptions of who does most crime might generate demands for the alleviation of poverty or redistribution of wealth. But the discussion participants rejected all forms of determinism, including those implicit in *Blocked Opportunities*. (Note that even when participants expressed positive versions of *Blocked Opportunities* they tended to do so by depicting offenders as *innovators,* that is, as rational, calculating actors).

If the participants view crime as disproportionately the work of poor people or members of minority groups and at the same time reject interpretations that focus on economic hardship, what then? The *logical* implication is that poor people are disproportionately morally inferior. And, of course, if poor people seem to be morally inferior, then poverty will not seem to be so much an evil as a condition that is well deserved (cf. Gans, 1988; Reiman, 1990; Scheingold, 1991).

Probably sensing these implications, many participants argued that crime is *not* disproportionately the work of poor people or members of minority groups. "Crime is everywhere," they sometimes insisted. But these defensive claims fly in the face of participants' accounts of their fears and behaviors. Recall that in response to the Stuart question, many self-critically admitted to subscribing to the "stereotype" of the black male offender. Recall as well that many told of avoiding certain neighborhoods or blocks that they regarded as particularly dangerous. All this is not to say that attention to crime will necessarily or universally cause people to regard in-the-flesh members of the putative underclass as morally inferior or deserving of their status. Rather, it is to suggest that such an outcome is a distinct possibility as it follows logically from the manner in which people talk about crime.

Culture Wars

The dominant frames *Faulty System* and *Social Breakdown* bolster imagery associated with the conservative position in what political analysts call the "culture war" (Hunter, 1992). At a general level of abstraction, these frames attribute crime to failures of social control, formal and informal; in effect, to *permissiveness*. Their prognostic components call for reassertions of authority—state, community, parental, and patriarchal. These images are broadly resonant with opposition to many of the new social movements, including feminism, gay liberation and abortion rights. It is therefore likely that attention to crime, because of the manner in which the issue tends to get constructed, will strengthen the conservative positions on a range of so-called cultural or social issues.

Spill-over Effects

Finally, and this point is closely related to the two previous points— there is the likelihood of a spill-over effect from crime to other issues. Because crime is a dominant issue on the public agenda, the frames that are used to interpret it are handy for use in interpreting other issues that can be construed as related. To the extent this is so, variations on *Social Breakdown* can be used to interpret the problems of poverty, unemployment, drug abuse, health care, infant mortality, and so on. This tendency is already occasionally evident in the rhetoric of conservative intellectuals. By way of example, consider former Attorney General William Barr's explanation for poverty: "[F]amily breakdown is a moral catastrophe and is at the root of so many of the problems that beset our nation. In my view, the root cause of both crime and poverty is precisely this unraveling of the family" (Barr, 1992). Because of the continuing salience of crime, and hence of the frames used most frequently to interpret it, I suspect that analyses of this type will become more common. Other urban social ills will therefore increasingly be constructed as essentially problems of breakdown and order rather than problems of inequality and social justice.

AGAINST THE TIDE

I have explained what I regard to be the political and public policy consequences of crime's prominent place in American public life. I want now to make a normative argument against standing idly by as these consequences develop. In so doing I necessarily exchange the role of disinterested observer for that of a claimsmaker.

In my view, criminal justice expansion is both futile and harmful. It is futile insofar as it has demonstrably failed to make the society markedly safer. Over the past twenty years, arrest rates have skyrocketed, most states have instituted mandatory prison terms for drug offenders, the death penalty has been reinstated and sentences for a wide variety of offenses have grown longer. As a result of these "get tough" measures, the United States has earned the dubious distinction of incarcerating a larger share of its population than any record keeping nation except Russia. Yet crime rates almost everywhere remain either stable or have declined only slightly. Moreover, as Currie (1985) points out, even if small gains can be accomplished through increasing punitiveness, they are accomplished at great social and financial cost and do not bring the society significantly closer to genuine civility.

Criminal justice expansion is also harmful in and of itself. For one thing, the courts, juvenile detention centers and prisons are rapidly becoming a primary institution for the socialization of young minority men. (The comparative importance of prisons versus college is already easy enough to assess: In 1992, more African American men were incarcerated in the former than enrolled in the latter [Mauer, 1994].) What will be the long-term effects of this state of affairs? In truth, it is difficult to say as our society has no experience with a criminal justice system of the proportions of the one we now have. Among African American young men, however, the *likely* effects include increased feelings of marginality and resentment; ironically, emotions of this sort many observers identify as major causes of crime (Braithwaite, 1989; Katz, 1988). In practical terms, their frequent involvement with the criminal justice system will certainly continue to undermine their ability to find such work as is available and to sustain family and community relationships.

There are at least two more reasons why criminal justice expansion of the sort we are witnessing is intrinsically harmful. First, rapidly rising criminal justice spending at all levels of government is increasingly crowding out spending for education, health care and housing (Chambliss, 1994). Law enforcement is thus replacing social welfare as the primary means by which the state manages the poor. Second, efforts by state and federal legislators to appear tough have resulted in grotesquely punitive sentences for relatively minor drug offenses. As a result, it is increasingly common for even small time drug dealers—including those whose wares consist only of marijuana—to receive lengthy prison sentences including life without any possibility for parole (Schlosser, 1994; Kaminer, 1994).

Those who have studied the politics of crime are understandably pessimistic about the possibilities for progressives on the issue. Stuart Hall and his colleagues write: "It is, perhaps, in relation to crime more than any other single area that the liberal voice is most constrained; that conventional definitions are hardest to resist; that alternative definitions are hardest to come by" (1978:90). Diana Gordon, in explaining her prediction that law and order approaches to crime will continue to pre-empt all others, writes:

> No countervailing symbols to the myth of crime and punishment have been found, no effective language of opposition to the individual perspective on remedies for crime. The values of tolerance, social protection and brotherly love are currently no match for the justifiable fear and outrage over street crime and the law and order politics that exploits them. (1990:41)

The situation for progressives is indeed bleak. *Blocked Opportunities* and *Racist System* are central to the progressive interpretation of crime yet both perform relatively poorly in the public discourse and in the discourse of regular people. Nevertheless, progressives must do their best to advance arguments of the sort I've laid out against attempts to reduce crime through ever more expansive and punitive criminal justice measures. In addition, in concluding the book, I offer a few words of advice on what else progressives should and should *not* say about crime.

A STRATEGY FOR PROGRESSIVES

Progressives should avoid advancing the unqualified claim that poverty causes crime. As noted above, the claim flies in the face of people's personal knowledge of individuals who have lifted themselves out of poverty without breaking the law. Moreover, as many people interpret it, it also implies the unacceptable notions that individual efforts to be good do not matter, and that poor people are *morally inferior* (this is ironic insofar as the supposition of moral inferiority is made tenable only through the *rejection* of *Blocked Opportunities*). The claim that poverty causes crime, so natural on the political Left, thus strikes many people as itself *immoral*. This does not mean, of course, that progressives should abandon all efforts to frame the problem of crime in structural terms; doing so, after all, would be tantamount to abandoning a central principle of progressive criminology. So what can progressives say about crime?

The urbanites in this study argued that the American moral order is unraveling; that people are increasingly out for themselves; that discipline and morality are fast disappearing. But they did not share a common analysis of the sources of societal unraveling. Indeed, though they routinely discussed the "breakdown" of family and community, they almost never tried to identify the sources of breakdown. Conservative intellectuals, of course, attribute societal unraveling to the "question authority" ethos of the new social movements and to the effects of government-sponsored social welfare programs. But the discussion participants rarely mentioned either. In my reading of the data, there is little *ideological depth* to popular feelings about moral breakdown and societal unraveling.

In the future, the symbolic contest over crime will likely focus on just this state of affairs; it will be a contest over how to understand the roots of social breakdown (the reality—not the frame). Progressives are in a good position to join this debate. They should vigorously challenge the notion that moral, familial and community decline stem from either antipoverty initiatives or progressive social movements (see Wilson, 1987; Currie, 1985). Instead, they should make the case that economic insecurity, poverty and racial discrimination *strain morality* and *disrupt families and communities*. Progressives, in other words, should attempt to reframe the crime debate in terms of a liberal version of *Social Breakdown*. Such an argument is advanced in the objectivist language of social science in Wilson's (1987) study of the urban underclass and in Currie's books on crime (1985) and drugs (1993). Not only does it have analytical merit, but because it begins with a recognition of *moral crisis*, it is also the argument most likely to resonate with a significant portion of the public.

In addition to attempting to reframe the crime debate, progressives should continue to push for public initiatives aimed at providing activities and opportunities for children. Such initiatives should improve public education and create staffed parks, youth centers, and street worker, athletic and after school programs. As much as the discussion participants argued that the criminal justice system should "get tough," they insisted that "activities" for children should be expanded. On this point, at least, there is apparently no gap between the views of progressives and those of a significant segment of the urban population.

Finally, at the local level, progressives should offer their support to neighborhood crime watch programs. Some Left critics charge that crime watch is part of the criminal justice system's expansion and penetration of communities (Gordon, 1990; Cohen, 1985; Elias, 1993). They argue that it contributes to the militarization of public spaces (Davis, 1992) and that it is potentially a mechanism for keeping blacks out of white neighborhoods (Rosenbaum, 1987). This study is not the proper venue for a thorough response to these criticisms, but I will say this: The notion that crime watch is part of the "net widening" of the criminal justice system is unfounded. In practice, crime watchers are simply not typically appendages of the state. They frequently criticize politicians, police and the courts, and in fact sometimes serve as a source of trouble for all three. Progressives should understand that as a form of collective action, crime watch is ultimately devoid of political content. Whether or not particular crime watch groups act in a fashion that abets criminal justice expansion or encloses public space depends on the ideological orientations of their members and key organizers.

Crime watch is best viewed as a form of what Donald Black (1988) calls "self help." It is a democratic and participatory alternative to state and private (e.g., security guards, alarm systems, flight from the city) "solutions." Moreover, many crime watchers form their groups as a means of fostering neighborhood solidarity. They sponsor clean ups, picnics and activities for neighborhood children. They use their groups as springboards for neighborhood associations that press more general concerns. And they frequently report increased commitment to their neighborhood as a result of the crime watch group.

There is another, more obvious reason to support crime watch. While the findings of evaluation research on crime watch programs are inconclusive (see Skogan, 1990), ample anecdotal evidence indicates that participants in densely populated neighborhoods can be effective in discouraging drug dealers and intervening to preempt muggings and assaults. Even where such intervention is too late to stop a mugging, it is often in time to restore the victim's faith in humanity, often among the more enduring casualties of street crime.

NOTES

1.   On the construction of categories of people (such as parents or neighbors) as either victims or victimizers, see Loseke, 1993.

2.   Throughout the heyday of the civil rights and student anti-war movements, the inclination to displace anxiety over rapid social change onto crime was encouraged by conservative politicians. Barry Goldwater, Spiro Agnew and George Wallace, among others, conflated social protest with crime and decried the general state of "lawlessness." Agnew, for example, described "troublemakers" as "muggers and criminals in the streets, assassins of political leaders, draft evaders and flag burners, campus militants, hecklers and demonstrators against candidates for public office and burners of cities" (Gordon, 1990:174).

SCHEDULE OF PEER GROUP
DISCUSSION QUESTIONS

Question 1

Here's the first question. What crimes are you most concerned about and who do you think is doing them?

Question 2

Here's the second question. In general, would you say the crime problem is getting worse or better, and why?

Question 3

Next I'm going to read three statements about crime. After each one, please tell me whether you agree strongly, agree somewhat, or disagree, and why.

Statement 1

Crime stems from the failure of the criminal justice system to apprehend and punish offenders. It's no wonder there's so much crime, criminals know that they can do whatever they please and get away with it! If we're serious about fighting crime then the police need to do a better job apprehending criminals, and the courts need to "get tough." Only when more criminals are made to do "hard time" will the message get out that "crime does not pay."

Statement 2

Crime stems from poverty, unemployment, poor education, bad housing, inadequate health care and discrimination. Inner-city kids turn to crime when they don't see any opportunities for legitimate work. If we're serious about fighting crime, we need to create more opportunities for disadvantaged kids. We'll only make progress in the fight against crime when we begin to seriously address these "root causes."

Statement 3

Crime stems from a breakdown of the traditional family and traditional community. In the past there was less crime because neighbors looked out for one another and parents supervised and disciplined their children. The best way to fight crime is for neighbors, in partnership with the police, to band together to restore order to their communities.

Question 4

We're ready to move on to question 4. Experts disagree about the best way to address the crime problem. In general, what do *you* think should be done in the City of Boston to reduce the amount of crime?

Question 5

There are two more questions. This next one is about crime watch. Why did you get involved in crime watch and what do you hope to accomplish?

Question 6

I have one last question. This one is going to require that you think back on something that happened in Boston several years ago. Do you all remember the Charles and Carol Stuart affair? In the few minutes that we have left, I'd like you to address this question: What effect did the Stuart affair have on the city of Boston? And what lessons, if any, should Bostonians learn from the Stuart affair?

CODING GUIDE

Note: An "n" after a code denotes the rebuttal or "negative" form of the idea element.

FAULTY SYSTEM

Crime stems from the failures of the formal agencies of social control. People do crimes because they believe they can get away with them. The solution to crime is to improve the performance of the criminal justice system. This frame has two subframes which specify the nature of the criminal justice system's failings.

Leniency. This subframe holds that the system is too lenient; sentences are too short; prison is too pleasant; judges are too lenient; laws protecting offenders place too many restrictions on police. The result is inadequate deterrence.

1.1 "Get tough" slogans and calls for the system to "crack down." For example: "If you can't do the time, don't do the crime." "No more coddling offenders!" [1.1n = general rejection of the "law and order" approach.]

1.2 Demands for expansion and more frequent administration of the death penalty. [These can be distinguished from calls for more *efficient* administration of the death penalty, which gets coded as Inefficiency].

1.3 Technicalities allow the guilty to go free and must therefore be eliminated. For example: the exclusionary rule; habeas corpus appeals; Miranda.

1.4 Harsh sentences are necessary as a form of "moral education." Retribution and public shaming are the proper purposes of the justice system.

1.5 Sentences are too short; they amount to a "slap on the wrist." Offenders should serve out their entire sentences; there should be "truth in sentencing"; plea bargaining and parole should be abolished. Prisons have "revolving doors."

1.6   Prison is a country club. Inmates should be made to work. Bring back the chain-gang. Get rid of the weights and color televisions. Get rid of the college scholarships. Make them "bust rocks."

1.7   The proper solution to overcrowding is to build more prisons or double/triple/quadruple bunk offenders. We *must* keep offenders locked up as long as necessary. [Emphasis here is on ensuring that offenders are locked up for as long as possible. Compare to 2.9]

1.8   Serious youthful offenders should be sentenced as adults. Youthful offenders should be fingerprinted. Youthful offenders get off too easily; they do crimes because they know they won't be punished.

1.9   Calls for a curfew; vagrancy laws; recriminalization of public drunkenness; use of the national guard for policing; or general anti-vagrancy "public order" type policing.

1.10   Politicians, judges, the powers that be, are permissive; they are reluctant to impose harsh sentences.

Inefficiency.   This subframe holds that the system is inefficient. First time offenders go free for lack of space; cases take too long to get to trial; offenders are "lost" in the shuffle. Deterrence suffers as a result. This frame is often implicit in statements that assume the solution to crime lies in a more efficient criminal justice system.

2.1   Due to the inefficiencies and inadequate resources of the criminal justice system, offenders are not getting apprehended and punished; hence the crime problem. (This general statement should be coded only if the more specific claims that follow do not yield a closer match). [2.1n = general rejections of the inefficiency subframe, as in, "The police can't reduce violence whose causes are social."]

2.2   The police department/court system is top-heavy; too much administration; too much bureaucracy.

2.3   Overcrowding means that some people are set free in order to make room for others, and that first offenders are rarely prosecuted. This undermines deterrence. The system must be made more certain.

2.4   Delays in getting defendants to trial and in punishment undermine deterrence. The system must be made more swift.

2.5   Inadequate funding for indigent defense aggravates prison overcrowding and precipitates early release. There must be adequate provision for indigent defense in order to ensure swiftness and certainty.

2.6   Parole and probation rolls are overcrowded; as a result, parolees/probationers are not being properly monitored. Violators are not being returned to prison. More probation/parole officers should be hired so that violators can be either put under more careful supervision or returned to prison.

2.7   Advocacy of intermediate sanctions (community service, electronic monitoring, boot camps, etc.) as a response to prison overcrowding *and* the resulting practice of early release. Intermediate sanctions can alleviate overcrowding while still administering punishment. [Note: Where alternative sentencing is supported for moral rehabilitation, code *Social Breakdown;* where it is supported for vocational training, code *Blocked Opportunities;* where multiple meanings are implied, use multiple codes.]

2.8   People do crimes because they know/believe nothing will happen to them. We need to do a better job *communicating* the risks of doing crimes.

2.9   We need to build more prisons to alleviate overcrowding *and* thereby restore the promise of imprisonment for criminal offenders. [Here the emphasis is on certainty of punishment rather than severity; compare to 1.7]

2.10   Praise for, or advocacy of a new policing strategy/program/ task force targeted at crime/drug dealing that seems promising. [Where advocacy of community policing includes calls for a "partnership," cross-code with *Social Breakdown.*]

2.11   Calls for hiring more cops or creating new policing agencies such as a "police corps." Calls for fire department patrols, and the use of city money to hire private security. Calls for budget increases for the police department.

2.12   Praise for, or advocacy of a new program/task force/strategy aimed at enhancing the performance of the court system.

BLOCKED OPPORTUNITIES

Crime stems from blocked opportunities, especially poverty, poor education, bad housing, lack of health care, unemployment and discrimination. The solution to crime is to ensure that everyone has the opportunity to escape poverty and achieve the "American Dream."

3.1   Attributions of crime to "hopelessness," or "despair." People
        do crimes because they do not see opportunities. People do
        crimes because of "anger" and "frustration." [These claims all
        focus on *perception* rather than underlying reality.]
3.2   Crime stems from discrimination or the accumulated effects of
        past discrimination.
3.3   Attribution for crime to "unemployment," "the economy," or
        "the recession." [3.3n = people do crimes because they don't
        want to work.]
3.4   Attribution for crime to "poverty," "deprivation," "despera-
        tion," "inequality."
3.5   For many people prison is not a deterrent because in terms of
        quality of life, it is an improvement. In prison you get three
        squares, heat and a roof over your head.
3.6   Housing project architecture is a cause of crime.
3.7   To reduce crime, the U.S. ought to spend more on job train-
        ing; job creation (e.g., the Civilian Conservation Corps); edu-
        cation; and welfare. [3.5n = claim that the social welfare
        programs of the "Great Society" are a source of crime.]
3.8   Advocacy of rehabilitation in the form of job training. Advo-
        cacy of intermediate sanctions where focus is on vocational
        training. [Moral rehabilitation gets coded as *Social Breakdown*.]
3.9   Advocacy of other types of social welfare programming such as
        Head Start, health care, housing, etc.
3.10   Crime stems from advertising's hard sell of consumer goods.
3.11   Street crime is poor people imitating the crimes of the power-
        ful in the only way available to them.

SOCIAL BREAKDOWN

Crime stems from a breakdown of informal social control. The breakdown of the traditional family and neighborhood has loosened the controls that used to keep people on the straight and narrow. Parents and
neighbors are no longer disciplining their children, teaching them the
right values, and supervising their behavior. The solution to crime lies in
instilling in young people proper values and restoring families and communities. There are liberal and conservative versions of the frame:

In the liberal version, breakdown is treated as a consequence of inequality, poverty, and, especially, joblessness. In other words, in the liberal version *Social Breakdown* gets conflated with *Blocked Opportunities*. 4.12
is the general code for the liberal version of the frame.

In the conservative version of this frame, breakdown is treated as a result of: (a) the decline of religion; (b) permissiveness engendered by the new social movements; (c) indolence engendered by the social welfare system. 4.7–4.11 are conservative versions of the frame.

Note: Discourse on "community policing" only gets cross-coded as *Social Breakdown* if the writer calls for a "police-community partnership."

4. Attributions for crime to community disintegration or family breakdown.

4.1 Crime stems from the proliferation of single parent families.

4.2 Parents used to do a better job raising their children (socializing children; instilling moral values in children).

4.3 Neighbors used to look out for one another; used to have "spanking rights" for neighborhood kids. This too usually gets expressed as a personal experience narrative. Typical is the claim that kids who did wrong used to get punished twice, once by the neighbor, then again upon returning home.

4.4 Personal experience narrative about a beat cop remembered from childhood *if* emphasis of narrative is on the cop's role as an *informal* agent of neighborhood control.

4.5 Urbanization fosters anonymity and hence crime. Kitty Genovese. Crime watch helps create social networks that compensate for erosion of traditional ties.

4.6 Crime stems from absence of role models.

4.7 The welfare system encourages out-of-wedlock pregnancies and divorce, and hence the formation of single-parent families. It is therefore a cause of crime.

4.8 Absence of religious training causes crime. Decline of the church is a source of crime.

4.9 There is a general decline in authority at home, in church, at school. We need to return to respecting traditional authority.

4.10 Because by law the police can no longer keep undesirables off the streets, neighborhood residents must take on this job.

4.11 Parents should be held accountable for their kids' crimes. They should be prosecuted and fined or even jailed if their kids are repeat offenders.

4.12 Poverty, unemployment, inequality, etc., disrupt family and community life and thereby engender crime.

4.14 Schools should engage in moral education.

4.15 Advocacy of rehabilitation programs if focus is on moral education.

4.16 Advocacy of street worker/youth counseling programs if emphasis is on moral guidance. Advocacy of parent-counseling programs.

4.17   Advocacy of creation of better recreational facilities if purpose is to keep young people occupied and supervised.

4.18   Advocacy of citizen anticrime activism: neighbors ought to take back their streets; take back the night. Advocacy of crime watch and related activities. One person might not be able to do much, but an organized bloc can work miracles. [4.18n = for example: "The physical risks are too great to expect citizens to patrol their own neighborhoods or drive off drug dealers."]

4.19   The idea of striking a "partnership" between community residents, the police, and the city government to eradicate crime. Cops can work with residents to create strategies for driving out prostitution, drug dealing. [This gets cross-coded with *Inefficiency*. It gets coded as *Social Breakdown* because, in addition to police action, it also emphasizes informal social control.] [4.19n = crime watch is a strategy foisted upon the people by officials whose true aim is to pass the buck. Fighting crime should *not* be the job of civilians but professionals.]

MEDIA VIOLENCE

Crime stems from violence in the movies, on television, and in music. The average teenager has witnessed 100,000 murders on television by age 18. Violence on television cheapens human life. It makes violence appear an acceptable way of responding to conflict. Life imitates art. The solution to the crime problem must involve some controls on violence in the media.

5.1   The routine depiction of violence on television makes it seem like acceptable behavior. By age 18, the average kid has seen 100,000 killings on television.

5.2   Violence in the media desensitizes people; it cheapens life.

5.3   Misogyny in rap makes violence against women seem acceptable.

5.4   Technological innovation in the mass media and the expansion of media markets are a source of crime.

5.5   The name of an offending show or band, e.g., 2 Live Crew or *Miami Vice*.

5.6   The cop shows and television glamorize the criminal lifestyle.

RACIST SYSTEM

The criminal justice system is racist; police target African American men for pat downs and harassment; judges sentence African Americans unfairly. The death penalty is administered in a racist fashion. In one version of this frame, crime control in the U.S. is depicted as part of a general conspiracy to eliminate young black men.

6.1 Police fail to properly patrol black communities. This double standard increases violence in black communities.

6.2 Police violate Fourth Amendment rights of African Americans through coerced confessions, illegal searches, frame-ups, and brutality. Rodney King. [This code should only be used in connection with discourse about African Americans; general discourse on Fourth Amendment protections gets codes as part of *Faulty System*.]

6.3 The stereotype of the black male criminal encourages some young black men to act out the role.

6.4 Racism and police brutality generate frustration among young African Americans and hence crime.

6.5 Justice is not blind. The police are more apt to arrest and the judges to jail black people than white. Blacks receive harsher/longer sentences.

6.6 Conspiracy of silence. This is the weak version of the conspiracy argument: Police and politicians ignore the fact that drugs come from "outside the community," that the big-time dealers are whites, and that most drug purchasers and users are suburban whites.

6.7 Genocidal conspiracy: This is the strong version of the conspiracy argument. Some organized entity is orchestrating the flooding of black communities with guns and drugs in order to eradicate young black men.

6.8 The only long-term solution to crime is racial justice.

6.9 The death penalty is administered in a racist fashion.

MEDIA DISCOURSE RESOURCES

This list includes all ideational material coded in the discussion transcripts as instances of Media Discourse.

FAULTY SYSTEM

Catch phrases:

Prisons have revolving doors.
Crime victims are victimized twice.
The system is set up to protect the rights of offenders not victims.
Police are handcuffed.
Offenders are released on technicalities.
No one wants a prison in her backyard.
If you do the crime you should do the time.

Spotlighted Facts, Positive

Prisons are overcrowded, necessitating double bunking/early release.
Communities try to keep prisons out of their "backyards."
Offenders are often released before their terms are up.
Offenders frequently plea bargain.
Prison costs $xxx amount per inmate per year.
Boot camps and electronic monitoring as alternatives to incarceration.
Sentences are random/not uniform.
A person must be arrested multiple times before seeing jail.
Abusive men violate restraining orders.
Boston is launching a community policing program.

Spotlighted Facts, In Rebuttal

Effects of mandatory minimum sentences.
Crime rates have not come down in spite of prison building boom.
The U.S. has the highest incarceration rates in the world.

BLOCKED OPPORTUNITIES

Catch phrases:

Underclass.

Spotlighted Facts:

Deindustrialization has undermined job prospects for many.
The minimum wage is not a living wage.
Reagan budget cuts generated crime.

Day care and child care for the poor are inadequate.
Crime stems from the emergence of an "underclass."
Job opportunities for young people are inadequate.
Unlike Europeans, Americans have no family leave policy.
Health care is too costly and unavailable to many.

Public Figures:

Michael Milken (in rebuttal)

SOCIAL BREAKDOWN

Catch phrases:

Family values
Single parent families.
Babies having babies
Take back the streets/take back the night.

Spotlighted Facts:

Proliferation of single mothers.
High divorce rates.
Neighborhoods in the past were more class-integrated.

Public Figures:

Kitty Genovese
Ozzie and Harriet Nelson

RACIST SYSTEM

Spotlighted Facts:

African Americans kill one another at higher rates than whites.

Public Figures:

Rodney King
David Duke

CRIME WATCH IN BOSTON

The following description of the Boston Police Department's Neighborhood Crime Watch Program (NCWP) is excerpted from the program's occasional newsletter, *Neighborhood Observer* (1992):

> The Neighborhood Crime Watch Program has assisted in the formation of 595 crime watch groups to date. Each of these 595 crime watches is a small group made up of the people on one street, or even just one block. It is very important to "think small," because the most crucial aspect of a crime watch group is the link from neighbor to neighbor.
> One of our coordinators will attend a meeting held in someone's home on the street. We provide meeting notices to the host to distribute to neighbors. At the first few meetings we help the group to:
> 1. Identify the specific crime issues on the street and ensure that neighbors are informed of them
> 2. Establish a telephone network among neighbors
> 3. Learn to rely on one another when traveling to and from their homes, and to respond effectively to a signal for help
> 4. Establish procedures for contacting police regarding incidents and how to follow up
> 5. Take control of street lighting, trash, shrub-trimming and other maintenance issues
> 6. Adopt basic home security measures
> 7. Learn the skills an attitudes to operate as an organized and empowered crime watch
>
> Afterwards, a group has the tools to be an effective crime watch. Residents can tailor these skills to meet the specific needs of their street. By monitoring crime incidents it will become apparent when or where to be especially vigilant. Clearly a crime watch will not completely eliminate crime, but an effective group does deter crime and reduce fear. A strong crime watch neighborhood is one that is very hard for a criminal to pass through unnoticed. Neighbors who are trained to react make their street inhospitable to someone intent on committing a crime.

The NCWP organizers report that most participants in crime watch meetings—as many as 75%—are female. This fact reflects a more general pattern. Manuel Castells (1983:68) attributes the overrepresentation of women in urban social movements to a "hierarchy of social tasks," deeply rooted in history, in which "Men took on the state and left the care of civil society to women."

Finally, the groups organized by the NCWP follow different paths of development. It is useful to distinguish three typical paths. The first includes groups that, after getting organized, continue to meet but restrict their activities to crime prevention. At their occasional meetings, such groups typically exchange information about the neighborhood, update telephone contact lists, and discuss strategies for enhancing security. The second includes groups that branch out from crime watch to sponsor other types of activities such as neighborhood clean ups, picnics, job fairs, block parties and so forth. Some groups which pursue this path eventually metamorphose into full-fledged neighborhood associations. The third includes groups that cease to meet regularly after starting up but in the minds of their members remain in existence. Members of groups of this type typically describe their crime watch as "dormant" but insist that it could be easily activated should the need arise.

REFERENCES

Althusser, Louis. 1971. "Ideology and Ideological State Apparatuses," Pp. 121–73 in *Lenin and Philosophy and Other Essays*. London: New Left Books.

Anderson, Elijah. 1990. *Streetwise*. Chicago: University of Chicago Press.

Barr, William P. 1992. "Crime, Poverty and the Family." *The Heritage Lectures*. Washington, DC: The Heritage Foundation.

Beccaria, Cesare. 1963. *On Crimes and Punishment*. Indianapolis, IN:Bobbs-Merrill Company.

Becker, Howard. 1963. *The Outsiders*. Glencoe, IL: The Free Press.

Beckett, Katherine. 1995. "Media Depictions of Drug Abuse: The Impact of Official Sources." *Journal of Research in Political Sociology*, forthcoming.

———. 1994a. *Crime and Drugs in Contemporary American Politics*. Unpublished Doctoral Dissertation. University of California at Los Angeles.

———. 1994b. "Setting the Public Agenda: 'Street Crime' and Drug Use in American Politics." *Social Problems* 41(3):425–47.

Beirne, Piers. 1993. *Homo Criminalis*. Stony Brook, NY: State University of New York Press.

Bellah, Robert N., Richard Madsen, William M. Sullivan, Ann Swidler, and Steven M. Tipton. 1985. *Habits of the Heart:* New York: Harper and Row.

Bennett, W. Lance. 1990. *Public Opinion in American Politics*. New York: Harcourt, Brace, Javanovich.

Best, Joel. 1990. *Threatened Children*. Chicago: University of Chicago Press.

Billig, Michael. 1991. *Ideology and Opinions*. Newbury Park, CA: Sage.

———. 1987. *Arguing and Thinking*. Cambridge, U.K.: Cambridge University Press.

Black, Donald. 1989. *Sociological Justice*. New York: Oxford University Press.

Blumer, Herbert. 1948. "Public Opinion and Public Opinion Polling." *American Sociological Review* 13:542–54.

Bortner, M.A. 1984. "Media Images and Public Attitudes Toward Criminal Justice," In Ray Surette, ed., *Justice and the Media*. Springfield, IL: Charles C. Thomas, Publisher.

Boston Police Department (B.P.D.). 1992. Office of Strategic Planning and Policy Development, Boston, MA.

Bouza, Anthony V. "We are the Enemy." *In These Times*, December 27, 1993.

Braithwaite, John. 1989. *Crime, Shame and Reintegration*. New York: Cambridge University Press.

Carbaugh, Donal. 1989. *Talking American*. Norwood, NJ: Abex Publishing Corporation.

Carlson, James M. 1985. *Prime Time Law Enforcement*. New York: Praeger.

Castells, Manuel. 1983. *The City and the Grassroots*. Berkeley: University of California Press.

Chambliss, William J. 1994. "Policing the Ghetto Underclass: The Politics of Law and Law Enforcement." *Social Problems* 41(2):177–94.

Cohen, Stanley. 1985. *Visions of Social Control*. Cambridge, U.K.: Polity Press.

Cohen, Stanley and Jock Young. 1981. *The Manufacture of News: Deviance, Social Problems and the Mass Media*. London: Constable.

Collins, Patricia. 1990. *Black Feminist Thought*. Cambridge, MA: Unwin Hyman, Inc.

Cullen, Francis T., and Gregory A. Clark, John B. Cullen an Richard A. Mathers. 1985. "Attribution, Salience and Attitudes Toward Criminal Sanctioning." *Criminal Justice and Behavior* 12(3):305–31.

Currie, Elliott. 1993. *Reckoning*. New York: Hill and Wang.

———. 1985. *Confronting Crime*. New York: Pantheon.

Davis, Mike. 1992 (originally 1990). *City of Quartz*. New York: Vintage.

Dahrendorf, Ralf. 1985. *Law and Order*. Boulder, CO: Westview Press.

Derber, Charles, William A. Schwartz and Yale Magrass. 1990. *Power in the Highest Degree*. New York: Oxford University Press.

Durkheim, Emile. 1964. *The Division of Labor in Society*. New York: Free Press.

Edelman, Murray. 1988. *Constructing the Political Spectacle*. Chicago: University of Chicago Press.

———. 1977. *Political Language*. New York: Academic Press.

Edsall, Thomas Byrne. 1991. *Chain Reaction*. New York: Norton.

Elias, Robert. 1993. *Victims Still*. Newbury Park, CA: Sage Press.

Elmendorf, Thomas. 1976. "Violence on TV." *Vital Speeches of the Day* 42(24):764–67.

Ericson, Richard V., Patricia M. Baranek, and Janet B. L. Chan. 1991. *Representing Order*. Toronto: University of Toronto Press.

Gallup, George. *The Gallup Poll Monthly*. 1989. Wilmington, Deleware: Scholarly Resources Press.

Gamson, William A. 1992. *Talking Politics*. New York: Cambridge University Press.

———. 1988. "A Constructionist Approach to Mass Media and Public Opinion." *Symbolic Interaction* 11(2):161–74.

Gamson, William A. and Andre Modigliani. 1989. "Media Discourse and Public Opinion on Nuclear Power," *American Journal of Sociology* 95:1–37.

———. 1987. "Changing Culture of Affirmative Action." *Research in Political Sociology* 3:137–77.

Gamson, William A., David Croteau, William Hoynes, and Theodore Sasson. 1992. "Media Images and the Social Construction of Reality." *Annual Review of Sociology* 18:373–93.

Gans, Herbert. 1988. *Middle American Individualism*. New York: Oxford University Press.

————. 1979. *Deciding What's News*. New York:Pantheon.

Gerbner, George and Larry Gross. 1976. "Living with Television: The Violence Profile." *Journal of Communication* 26:172–99.

Gerbner, George, Larry Gross, Michael Morgan, and Nancy Signorielli. 1980. "The 'Mainstreaming' of America: Violence Profile No. 11." *Journal of Communication* 30:10–29.

Gitlin, Todd. 1980. *The Whole World is Watching*. Berkeley, CA: University of California Press.

Goffman, Erving. 1974. *Frame Analysis*. Cambridge, MA: Harvard University Press.

Gordon, Diana. 1990. *The Justice Juggernaut*. New Brunswick, NJ: Rutgers University Press.

Graber, Doris. 1980. *Crime News and the Public*. New York: Praeger.

Gubrium, Jaber F. 1993. "For a Cautious Naturalism," Pp. 55–67 in Gale Miller and James Holstein, eds., *Constructionist Controversies*. Hawthorne, NY: Aldine de Gruyter.

Gusfield, Joseph R. 1981. *The Culture of Public Problems*. Chicago: University of Chicago Press.

Hall, Stuart, Charles Critcher, Tony Jefferson, John Clarke, and Bran Roberts. 1978. *Policing the Crisis*. London: Macmillan.

Hunter, James Davison. 1992. *Culture Wars*. New York: Basic Books.

Ibarra, Peter and John Kitsuse. 1993. "Vernacular Constituents of Moral Discourse: An Interactionist Proposal for the Study of Social Problems," Pp. 21–54 in Gale Miller and James A. Holstein, eds., *Constructionist Controversies*. Hawthorne, N.Y.: Aldine de Gruyter.

Iyengar, Shanto. 1991. *Is Anyone Responsible?* Chicago: University of Chicago Press.

Jay, Martin. 1973. *The Dialectical Imagination*. Boston: Little Brown.

Jencks, Christopher. 1992. *Rethinking Social Policy*. New York: Harper Collins.

Jhally, Sut and Justin Lewis. 1992. *Enlightened Racism*. Boulder, CO: Westview.

Johns, Christina Jacqueline. 1992. *Power, Ideology, and the War on Drugs*. New York: Praeger.

Katz, Jack. 1988. *Seductions of Crime*. New York: Basic Books.

Katzenbach, Nicholas.deB. 1968. "Violence." *Vital Speeches of the Day* 34(20):615–17.

Kaminer, Wendy. "Federal Offense." *The Atlantic Monthly*, June, 1994.

Komarnicki, Mary and John Doble. 1986. "Crime and Corrections: A Review of Public Opinion Data Since 1975." New York: The Public Agenda Foundation.

Lemert, Edwin M. 1972. *Human Deviance, Social Problems and Social Control*, Second Edition. Englewood Cliff, NJ: Prentice Hall.

Lewis, Dan A. and Greta Salem. 1986. *Fear of Crime*. New Brunswick, NJ: Transaction Books.

Lewis, Justin. 1991. *Ideological Octopus*. New York: Routledge.

Logan, John R. and Harvey L. Molotch. 1987. *Urban Fortunes*. Berkeley: University of California Press.

Loseke, Donileen R. 1993. "Constructing Conditions, People, Morality, and Emotion: Expanding the Agenda of Constructionism," Pp. 207–216 in Gale Miller and James A. Holstein, eds., *Constructionist Controversies*. Hawthorne, NY: Aldine de Gruyter.

Mauer, Mark. 1994. "Americans Behind Bars: The International Use of Incarceration." Washington, DC: The Sentencing Project.

Mayer, William G. 1992. *The Changing American Mind*. Ann Arbor: The University of Michigan Press.

McCombs, Maxwell, Edna Einsiedel and David Weaver. 1991. *Contemporary Public Opinion*. Hillsdale, NJ: Lawrence Earlbaum Associates.

Merton, Robert K. 1938. "Social Structure and Anomie," in *American Sociological Review* 3:672–82.

Miller, Gale and James A. Holstein. 1993. "Social Constructionism as Social Problems Work," Pp. 131–152 in Gale Miller and James A. Holstein, eds., *Constructionist Controversies*. Hawthorne, NY: Aldine de Gruyter.

Mills, C. Wright. 1959. *The Sociological Imagination*. New York: Oxford University Press.

Morgan, David L. 1988. *Focus Groups as Qualitative Research*. Newbury Park, CA: Sage.

Morley, David. 1986. *Family Television*. London: Routledge.

"Neighborhood Observer." 1992. Neighborhood Crime Watch Program (NCWP), Boston Police Department.

Neuman, Russell W., Marion R. Just, and Ann N. Crigler. 1992. *Common Knowledge: News and the Constructions of Political Meaning*. Chicago: University of Chicago Press.

Neuman, W. Russell. 1986. *The Paradox of Mass Politics*. Cambridge, MA: Harvard University Press.

Niemi, Richard G., John Mueller, and Tom W. Smith. 1989. *Trends in Public Opinion*. New York: Greenwood Press.

Nixon, Richard. 1973. "Law Enforcement and Drug Abuse Prevention." *Vital Speeches of the Day* 39(2):354–7.

Pfohl, Stephen. 1985. *Visions of Deviance and Social Control*. New York: McGraw Hill.

Potter, Jonathan and Margaret Wetherell. 1987. *Discourse and Social Psychology*. Newbury Park, CA: Sage.

Public Agenda Foundation (PAF). 1993. *Criminal Violence: What Direction Now for the War on Crime?* New York: McGraw-Hill.

Quinney, Richard. 1974. *Critique of the Legal Order*. Boston: Little Brown.

———. 1970. *The Social Reality of Crime*. Boston: Little Brown.

Reiman, Jeffrey. 1990. *The Rich Get Richer and the Poor Get Prison*. New York: Macmillan.

Reinharz, Shulamit. 1984. *On Becoming a Social Scientist*. New Brunswick, NJ: Transaction Publishers.

Reinarman, Craig and Harry G. Levine. 1989. "The Crack Attack: Politics and Media in America's Latest Drug Scare," Pp. 115–137 in Joel Best ed., *Images of Issues*. Hawthorne, NY: Aldine de Gruyter.

Roberts, Julian V. 1992. "Public Opinion, Crime, and Criminal Justice," Pp. 99–180 in Michael Tonry, ed., *Crime and Justice: A Review of Research*. Chicago: University of Chicago Press.

Rosenbaum, Dennis. 1987. "The Theory and Research Behind Neighborhood Watch: Is It a Sound Fear and Crime Reduction Strategy?" *Crime and Delinquency* 33:103–34.

Rubin, Lillian B. 1988. *Quiet Rage*. Berkeley, CA: University of California Press.

———. 1975. *Worlds of Pain*. New York: Basic Books.

Ryan, William. 1976. *Blaming the Victim*. New York: Vintage.

Sasson, Theodore. 1995. "African American Conspiracy Theories and the Social Construction of Crime." *Sociological Inquiry* 65(3).

Scheingold, Stuart. 1991. *The Politics of Street Crime*. Philadelphia, PA: Temple University Press.

———. 1984. *The Politics of Law and Order*. New York: Longman.

Schlosser, Eric. "Marijuana and the Law." *The Atlantic Monthly*, September, 1994.

Schutz, Alfred. 1967. *The Phenomenology of the Social World*. Evanston, IL: Northwestern University Press.

Skogan, Wesley G. 1990. *Disorder and Decline*. Berkeley, CA: University of California Press.

Smith, Robert C. and Richard Selzer. 1992. *Race Class and Culture*. Albany, NY: State University of New York Press.

Snow, David A. and Robert Benford. 1988. "Ideology, Frame Resonance, and Participant Mobilization." *International Social Movement Research* 1:197–217.

Snow, David A., E. Burke Rochford, Jr., Steven K. Worden, and Robert D. Benford. 1986. "Frame Alignment Processes, Micromobilization, and Movement Participation." *American Sociological Review* 51:464–81.

Stacey, Judith. 1991. *Brave New Families*. New York: Basic Books.

Stinchcombe, A. L. and R. Adams, C.A. Heimer, K.L. Schepple, T.W. Smith, and D.G. Taylor. 1980. *Crime and Punishment: Changing Attitudes in America*. San Francisco: Josey-Bass.

Sutherland, Edwin. 1955 (Revised by Donald Cressey). *Principles of Criminology* (5th Edition). Philadelphia, PA: Lippincott.

Swidler, Ann. 1986. "Culture in Action: Symbols and Strategies." *American Sociological Review* 51:273–86.

Tuchman, Gaye. 1978. *Making News*. New York: The Free Press.

U.S. Department of Justice, Bureau of Justice Statistics, Washington, DC: Press Release, March, 1995.

———. "Historical Corrections Statistics in the U.S., 1850–1984." December, 1986.

———. *Uniform Crime Report*, 1992.

Wachs, Eleanor. 1988. *Crime Victim Stories*. Bloomington, IN: Indiana University Press.

Wilson, James Q. 1983 (revised edition). *Thinking About Crime*. New York: Vintage.

———. "What To Do About Crime." *Commentary*, September, 1994.

Wilson, William J. 1987. *The Truly Disadvantaged*. Chicago: University of Chicago Press.

Op Eds Quoted in the Text

Clark, Kenneth B. "In Cities, Who is the Real Mugger?" *New York Times*, September 30, 1990.

Cohen, Richard. "Indignation to Apathy." *Washington Post,* May 24, 1991.

Domanick, Joe. "New York According to Charles Dickens." *Los Angeles Times,* November 5, 1990.

Fyfe, James J. "Why Won't Crime Stop?" *Washington Post,* March 17, 1991.

Glowacki, Janusz. "Sorry, I'm No Crime Fighter." *New York Times,* September 27, 1990.

Kinsley, Michael. "When the Constable Blunders." *Washington Post,* April 19, 1991.

Krauthammer, Charles. "Culture Has Consequences." *Washington Post,* October 26, 1990.

Lay, Donald P. "Our Justice System, So-Called." *The New York Times,* October 22, 1990.

Leshaw, Gary. "Giving Police Carte Blanche Poses a Threat." *Atlanta Constitution,* March 29, 1991.

Letwin, Michael Z. "Wrong Way to Fight Crime." *New York Times,* October 6, 1990.

Mokhiber, Russell. "Crime: The Shame of It All." *Washington Post,* October 28, 1990.

Murphy, Patrick T. "We Need Fewer Guns, More Individual Responsibility." *Chicago Tribune,* September 16, 1990.

Neely, Richard. "Law and Order—Do It Yourself." *Washington Post,* October 21, 1990.

Page, Clarence. "Police Brutality and the Vicious Cycle of Fear." *Chicago Tribune,* March 13, 1991.

Pillsbury, Samuel. "Speak Up, or the Criminals Win." *Los Angeles Times,* December 24, 1990.

Purdum, Todd. "Is There a Cheaper Way to Attack Rising Crime?" *New York Times,* September 23, 1990.

Rockwell, Llewellyn H. "It's Safe Streets Versus Urban Terror." *Los Angeles Times,* March 10, 1991.

Stark, Evan. "The Myth of Black Violence." *New York Times,* July 18, 1990.

Walton, Reggie B. "Making Life Easier for the District's Killers." *Washington Post,* October 21, 1990.

Watkins, Todd. "From the Watkins Family." *New York Times,* September 12, 1990.

Wicker, Tom. "Taking Aim at Fear." *New York Times,* September 16, 1990.

Will, George. "What Grandmother Took for Granted." *Washington Post,* February 14, 1991.

Yancey, Charles C. "Anti-Crime Partnership." *Boston Globe,* April 29, 1991.

Yocum, Susan. "Professionals, Not Clones in Blue." *Los Angeles Times,* September 11, 1990.

INDEX

Adams, R., 7, 22, 165
Agnew, Spiro, 6, 172
Alger, Horatio, 150
Althusser, Louis, 147

Baranek, Patricia M., 12
Barr, William P., 14, 168
Beccaria, Cesare, 29, 30, 34, 144
Becker, Howard, 106
Beckett, Katherine, 3, 5, 6, 8–9, 11, 14, 16, 19
Beirne, Piers, 30, 105
Bellah, Robert N., 150
Benford, Robert D., 10, 12
Bennett, Willie, 114, 121
Bennett, W. Lance, 19, 114, 121
Best, Joel, 2, 145–146
Billig, Michael, 19, 20, 141, 157
Black, Donald, 172
black male offender, stereotype of, 6, 9, 24, 111, 122, 145, 164, 167–8
Blocked Opportunities
  coding method, 91
  defined, 14–15, 18
  in the media discourse, 88–90
  in the popular discourse, 91–103
  origins, 87–8
  see also experiential knowledge;
    popular wisdom; media
    discourse
Blumer, Herbert, 19
Bortner, M. A., 12
Boston, 2
  demographic profile, 28
  neighborhoods, 20–21, 27, 28
Boston Police Department, 20, 114, 185

Bouza, Anthony V., 15
Braithwaite, John, 169
Bruck, David, 14–15
Burgess, Ernest, 55
Bush, George, 6, 14
Bush, Jeb, 165

Capone, Al, 88
Carbaugh, Donal, 150
Carlson, James M., 152
Castells, Manuel, 185
Chambliss, William J., 4–5, 128, 156, 166, 169
Chan, Janet B. L., 12
claimsmakers, 2, 169
Clark, Gregory A., 22
Clark, Kenneth B., 89—90
Clarke, John, 12, 84, 162, 170
class, influence on resource strategy, 154–6
Clinton, William J., 5, 15, 165
coding, 30, 36–7, 91
cognitive maps, 24, 28
Cohen, Richard, 57
Cohen, Stanley, 12, 171
Collins, Patricia, 157
community, discourse on, *see Social Breakdown*
conclusions, 161–72
conspiracy theories, 118–20, 124
constructionist explanation for crime
  discourse, 129–58, 162–5
  hypotheses, 129–30
constructionist paradigm, 2, 127
constructionist theory, 128–9
conventional wisdom, 3–4, 9, 52, 84, 104, 161–2, 165